IT IS DANGEROUS TO
BE RIGHT
WHEN THE
GOVERNMENT
IS WRONG

Also by Andrew P. Napolitano

Constitutional Chaos: What Happens When Government Breaks Its Own Laws

*The Constitution in Exile: How the Federal Government Has
Seized Power by Rewriting the Supreme Law of the Land*

A Nation of Sheep

Dred Scott's Revenge: A Legal History of Race and Freedom in America

Lies the Government Told You: Myth, Power, and Deception in American History

IT IS DANGEROUS TO
BE RIGHT
WHEN THE
GOVERNMENT
IS WRONG

THE CASE FOR PERSONAL FREEDOM

ANDREW P. NAPOLITANO

THOMAS NELSON
Since 1798

NASHVILLE   DALLAS   MEXICO CITY   RIO DE JANEIRO

Published in Nashville, Tennessee, by Thomas Nelson. Thomas Nelson is a registered trademark of Thomas Nelson, Inc.

Thomas Nelson, Inc., titles may be purchased in bulk for educational, business, fund-raising, or sales promotional use. For information, please e-mail SpecialMarkets@ThomasNelson.com.

Library of Congress Cataloging-in-Publication Data

Napolitano, Andrew P.
 It is dangerous to be right when the government is wrong : the case for personal freedom / by Andrew P. Napolitano.
   p. cm.
Includes bibliographical references and index.
 ISBN 978-1-59555-350-8 (alk. paper)
 1. Civil rights--United States. 2. Civil rights--Philosophy. 3. Liberty--Philosophy. 4. Natural law--Philosophy. I. Title.
 JC599.U5N25 2011
 323.0973--dc23
 2011019142

Printed in the United States of America
11 12 13 14 15 QGF 6 5 4 3 2 1

This book is dedicated to
Congressman Ron Paul,
Physician, Philosopher, Economist, Public Servant,
and Defender of the Constitution.
Through his tireless efforts,
Freedom itself
has been rekindled
in the hearts of millions of Americans.

"Our rulers will best promote the improvement of the people by strictly confining themselves to their own legitimate duties—by leaving capital to find its most lucrative course, commodities their fair price, industry and intelligence their natural reward, idleness and folly their natural punishment—by maintaining peace, by defending property, by diminishing the price of law and by observing strict economy in every department of the State. Let the government do this: The people will assuredly do the rest."

—THOMAS BABINGTON MACAULAY

"It is dangerous to be right when the government is wrong."

—VOLTAIRE

"Does the government exist to protect our freedoms, or do we exist to serve the government?"

—ANONYMOUS

"You have rights antecedent to all earthly governments; rights that cannot be repealed or restrained by human laws; rights derived from the Great Legislator of the Universe."

—PRESIDENT JOHN ADAMS

Contents

Chapter 8:

Chapter 9:

Chapter 10:

Chapter 11:

Chapter 12:

Chapter 13:

Chapter 14:

Chapter 15:

Author's Note

Is Freedom a Myth or Reality?

Does the government exist to serve us or to master us? If the government exists to serve us and if freedom is part of our humanity, how can the government take freedom from us? Is human freedom in America a myth, or is it reality?

In all my previous written works, I have emphasized the theme that all human beings possess natural rights as part of our humanity. In the Judeo-Christian tradition, we view these rights as gifts from our Creator. This is particularly so if you are an American, and if you mark the founding of this nation at July 4th 1776, as it was then that the Continental Congress promulgated in the Declaration of Independence Jefferson's immortal—though hardly novel—words to the effect that we humans are created equal and are endowed by our Creator with certain inalienable rights, and among these are life, liberty, and the pursuit of happiness. Historians have speculated that Jefferson originally planned to use the concept of property ownership in that iconic litany of human rights, but his fear of addressing slavery in the same document in which he had characterized the long train of abuses visited upon the colonists by the king of England, would have opened the Declaration and its signers to charges of hypocrisy.

Nevertheless, Talmudic and Christian scholars, and renowned skeptics, even atheists and deists, had long held, by Jefferson's time, that the divine right of kings was a myth, that all humans own their own bodies, and that personal freedoms are integral to those bodies. Whether the ultimate source of human freedom is found in theology or biology, freedom exists, freedom is ours by nature, and the long history of the world is really one unceasing, increasing catalogue of the epic battles for personal freedoms against tyranny.

Stated differently, I have argued in my work at Fox News, as a judge, as a lawyer, as an author, lecturer, and law school professor that our basic human liberties—thought, speech, press, worship, travel, privacy, association, self-defense, bodily integrity, dominion over ownership of property, fairness from the government, and the presumption of liberty at all times under all circumstances and in all conflicts—are the essence of humanity.

If you read the Bill of Rights—the first ten amendments of the Constitution—you will see that the theme of my other works, and of this book, was pretty much accepted by the Framers. As you will read recounted here, they, like I, were skeptical of Big Government. Some, like Patrick Henry and George Mason, were, like I am, skeptical of all government. The Framers viewed, as do I, the only legitimate role of government as protecting freedom. That connotes protection from force and fraud, but it surely does not connote punishing the politically unorthodox, transferring wealth, regulating personal private behavior, stealing property, or manipulating currency. I suspect that if you actually picked up this book and have read these introductory remarks up to this point, you will generally agree with me: So far so good.

Now the dark part: There is no human liberty, natural or constitutional, expressly guaranteed in the Constitution or traditionally viewed as belonging to all persons, that has not been nullified by the government in America. We are deluding ourselves if we really think that the government thinks that the so-called guarantees of freedoms are truly guarantees. They are not. They have been tolerated by American governments unless and until the governments feel threatened by them. Of course, a guarantee that can be suspended whenever those obligated on the guarantee no longer feel bound by it, is no guarantee whatsoever.

Throughout our history, persons in America have had all natural rights denied by different levels of government, from slavery to abortion, from punishment for speech to theft of property, from denial of due process to invasions of privacy; and the government has prevailed. This book is my sixth book. All have been unhappy discussions about the Constitution and the government's unrestrained willingness to disregard it.

This book, like its predecessors, tells the stories that generally do not have happy endings. Most of the times freedom loses. But these are arguments that come from my heart as well as my head; and they should resonate in your heart and head.

Every day in many a way, seen and unseen, liberty is lost. It is the purpose of this book to address the seen and the unseen, to argue for the primacy of the individual over the state, and to help foment a reawakening of the natural human thirst for freedom.

Come with me now on a wild ride through the annals of freedom in America; and as you read these pages, ask yourself if, at each turn, we are closer to freedom or slavery, if the majesty of the law really means what it says, and why—*why*—it is dangerous to be right when the government is wrong.

Introduction

Where Do Our Rights Come From?

After a trip to the American Midwest in 1959, Nikita Khrushchev, then the ruler of the Soviet Union, became convinced that corn could solve many of the USSR's economic woes. Russia had long struggled with miserably inadequate food supplies, the result of years of inept Communist agricultural policies. Having witnessed the wild success of corn production in America, Khrushchev reasoned that the grain could be equally successful in Russia, and thus support increased meat and dairy production necessary to feed the population. He therefore commanded that vast swaths of land, including the frigid tundra of Siberia, be converted to corn crops. As it turned out, corn was entirely unsuitable to the Russian climate, and the plan was a complete disaster.

The reason, of course, that the policy failed was Khrushchev's ignorance of the immutable fact—the self-evident truth—that corn can only be grown under certain conditions, and Russia's climate did not provide them. The cost of this misjudgment was wasted resources and prolonged hunger. It is obvious that politicians must enact laws which are in accord with such "truths." If they do not, then the inevitable consequence is human suffering. There are some things which humans and their constructed governments simply cannot change; that is to say, those things transcend our human capacities and cannot be the object of our will. Individuals and governments are thus always secondary and subject to these truths.

What are these truths, but "natural laws"? What other laws are there, with which human commands must accord? As we shall see, there are natural rights every human possesses by virtue of being human which protect our essential "yearnings" from government interference. And as we shall also see, man-made laws are only valid to the extent that they comport with and are subject to these natural rights. This is all known as the Natural Law.

This scheme is in contrast to the legal philosophy of Positivism, which says that laws need not pass any kind of moral muster to be considered valid. In other words, laws are purely "posited" by human beings, and governments are not constrained by principles such as human rights, fairness, and justice when making those laws. Not only is this philosophy that "law is whatever the government says it is" untrue, but it has facilitated mankind's biggest catastrophes and legitimized the most malevolent regimes in human history. Why were Hitler and his policies "evil"? After all, they were enacted by a popularly elected government that followed its own procedures to acquire power and enact lawful laws. Positivists have no answer to this question, because they cannot tell us *why* killing millions of innocent civilians is wrong: For Positivists, the Final Solution was just as valid as a law prohibiting jaywalking. Thus, under the Positivist scheme, our rights to life, liberty, and the pursuit of happiness are only as safe as our government would care to have them.

Why do we even care whether a law must comport with the Natural Law to be considered valid? After all, if the consequence of not obeying a law is imprisonment, then we will obey that law regardless of whether it is valid or not. The answer is because, like Khrushchev's corn plan, every time the government's commands flout the Natural Law, evil occurs, and we lose sight of the dream which our Founders enshrined for us in the Declaration of Independence and the Constitution. We must hold the government accountable for its violations of our natural rights if we are ever to have liberty. As Jefferson once said, "Eternal vigilance is the price of liberty." And as St. Augustine said and St. Thomas Aquinas taught, "An unjust law is no law at all."[1]

This Congress Hereby Declares Gravity to Be Illegal: It Is Too Much of a Downer

Before we can discuss what precisely the Natural Law encompasses, we must examine its basis in the Eternal Law. The Eternal Law can essentially be thought of as those laws which govern the functioning of the universe, such as the laws of physics, anatomy, chemistry, mathematics, and biology. These laws are imprinted into the very order and nature of things. As an example, molecules of water can only ever be comprised of two hydrogen atoms and one oxygen atom. Change that composition, and you no longer have water. Moreover, the laws of chemistry also dictate that when water is cooled to below thirty-two degrees Fahrenheit, its molecular structure shifts, and it turns into ice. Whether one thinks of these laws as scientific rules, or the product of the divine and infallible will of God, it cannot change the following: These "truths" are immutable, and the universe is and always will be subject to them.

Furthermore, these rules are self-evident, which is to say that although we may attempt to understand their workings, their truthfulness requires no explanation or proof. When humans study science, they are essentially trying to recognize and explain those rules to which we are subject, and thus be able to predict the future outcome of an interaction between two or more "things." The field of medicine, for example, tries to understand how a bacterial infection will respond to a particular antibiotic. If we do so, then we can know when and under what circumstances a particular antibody should be prescribed to restore the body to its normal, healthy state. We are therefore operating within the Eternal Law; and as any scientist will tell you, scientific rules don't change. Only man-made theories for what those rules are and how they operate may change.

However, without an explanation or understanding, those rules remain just as "true": Penicillin will combat certain infections, and gravity will always pull things toward the center of the earth, regardless of whether or not we understand how. In other words, explanation and human understanding cannot make those truths more "true": They rely on nothing human for their existence. If they did, then they would change along with all of the vagaries in taste and flaws in reasoning of the human mind. Thus, these laws transcend the temporal human mind and all of its imperfections. Although this may seem abstract now, it will make more sense when we explore other kinds of laws which do require an explanation for their truth, and a basis for their existence.

Consider what would happen if, based upon legislative findings that gravity was causing too many injuries to falling senior citizens, Congress declared that henceforth all things shall fall at a slower speed. Clearly, this would not change the way that matter interacts with gravity, and thus the manner in which the universe functions. Rather, it would just distort other (man-made) calculations of the force of gravity: Although gravitational force would no doubt be calculated at lower numbers due to Congress's laws, falling would hurt just as much. Consequently, we would sadly have just as many injured senior citizens as we did before, but we would have the illusion that Congress was doing something positive to protect seniors.

It would be equally ridiculous if Congress tried to declare that $2 + 2 = 22$, or by printing money, there was more "value" in an economy with which to purchase goods and services. As St. Thomas More's character states in Robert Bolt's play *A Man for All Seasons*, "Some men think the Earth is round, others think it flat; . . . . But if it is flat, will the King's command make it round? And if it is round, will the King's command flatten it? *No.*" Clearly, the Eternal Law is an absolute limit on the will and power of the government. Thus, it is another self-evident truth that humans can never alter, and are always trumped by, the eternal and natural laws, or if you prefer, God's laws and nature's laws, or as Jefferson said, "The Laws of Nature and of Nature's God."

The Yearnings of Mankind

St. Thomas Aquinas stated that the Natural Law was the role in which human beings play in the Eternal Law. The primary distinction between human beings and other objects of the Eternal Law is that we are in possession of reason and free will. As stated above, human beings are able to recognize self-evident truths about the world in which we live through observation and the application of reason to those observations. Thus if we go to bed at night and the ground is dry, and we observe the next morning that the dirt has turned into mud, we are able to reason that it rained during the night. Moreover, we exercise reason and free will in order to realize all of our fundamental human yearnings, such as life, liberty, and the pursuit of happiness. This inclination to reach a proper end (our yearnings) through the application of reason is the Natural Law; it is our human nature. Although this may all sound abstract, we experience this process on a daily basis: Since we have a human yearning to provide for ourselves and our loved ones, we have learned through the exercise of reason that we can best accomplish that "proper end" by going to work nearly every day. Thus, it is a fundamental human inclination to exert energy to meet one's natural needs. If we don't, we die.

This, of course, begs the question of what are those "proper ends" that God has dictated we as humans *naturally* strive for, or—for our secular readers—what nature has dictated that we instinctually strive for. Indeed, it is the perceived subjectivity of the answer to that question which has made Natural Law an unappealing philosophy to many. As was mentioned above, one of the traditional answers was "all of those things which we yearn for." To begin with, all living things strive for self-preservation. Thus, it is a natural inclination to consume food and water, and to defend oneself from attacks. However, as humans possess certain traits which are peculiar to themselves, there are additional "ends" which we do not share with other animals. For example, it is a natural yearning to love, to acquire knowledge, and to express oneself creatively. Those yearnings, however, do not lend themselves to being "listed." In fact, to do so is to tread into dangerous territory because if we only recognize those listed yearnings, then we are in danger of disparaging others that we leave out. As we shall discuss below, the Founders recognized this problem and provided a solution to it with the Ninth and Fourteenth Amendments.

Since I first read the Declaration of Independence as a high school student, I have been fascinated with the concept of self-evident truths. If we agree with the generally accepted definition of self-evident truths—those which do not require hard evidence in order to evince acceptance—we run into two problems. The first is that at some time there surely must have been some evidence that caused universal acceptance of these truths; as in, it is self-evident that the Sun rises in the east every morning because the ancients and we have seen it there; as in, every human being has material needs to stay alive because the ancients and we have gotten hungry and cold and awkward at nakedness; as in, all things are subject to the laws of cause and effect, except for the uncaused cause, whom believers call God and our secular colleagues call Nature. These observations of the Sun and realizations of our own self-needs are, in fact, evidence for their universal acceptance. But the universality of these "truisms" (another way of saying self-evident truths) allows us to dispense with the need to provide scientific evidence in support of them whenever we articulate them. Stated differently, no rational person can seriously challenge truisms when we use them as building blocks for our arguments.

The second problem we need to confront when commencing an argument with truisms is the realization that many people are willfully blind even to the obvious. Thus, while the truism that "all Men are created equal" may have been self-evident to the Founders[2], it surely was not self-evident to King George III or to the millions on the planet then and now to whom the divine right of kings provided and still provides a moral basis for tyranny. Moreover, it was not self-evident to the Founders themselves that "all Men are created equal" applied to all human beings, not solely to property-owning adult white males.

From the above we can conclude that not every person in every age is sufficiently exposed to the truth so as to recognize it. Because we are all fallen—that is, our human nature has inherited the imperfections of original sin—we do not always recognize a truism. This is so because the truth is often inconvenient, painful, and upsetting; and it requires rational thought, acceptance of revelation, and personal courage to pursue.

Jefferson's remarkable, radical insistence that "all Men are created equal" and are "endowed by their Creator" with certain "unalienable Rights" and that among those rights are "Life, Liberty, and the Pursuit of Happiness," and all these principles are "self-evident . . . Truths," was surely inconvenient, painful, and upsetting to many and hardly self-evident to the elites of his time. What about women, what about people of color, what about children, what about those without property: Why wasn't the self-evident truth of their equality and their natural rights recognized? And if the king didn't morally have all the power he claimed to have, how did the colonists come to occupy the land that he gave them via their predecessors? Even the most enlightened of men were blind to some truisms.

What does it take to peel away errors of willful blindness? It takes intellect and free will. That we all possess the free will to pursue the truth, the intellect to recognize and accept it, and that its pursuit is the ultimate goal of human activity, is the ultimate truism. There are many self-evident truths that all rational persons recognize. Some come from human reason (the Sun rising, our needs for food, shelter, and clothing, as examples), and some come from revelation (we have the rights to life, liberty, property, and happiness; it is wrong to lie, cheat, steal, and murder, as examples). Some come from reason and revelation (government is essentially the negation of liberty; humans have free immortal souls while governments are finite and based on coercion and force). But the concept of self-evident truths—or truisms—is absolutely essential to freedom. Truisms reject moral relativism, and American exceptionalism. They compel an understanding of the laws of nature that animate and regulate all human beings at all times, in all places, and under all circumstances. And truisms equal *freedom*.

Once we recognize those human yearnings, we can begin to understand the evil of government commands which infringe upon those yearnings. The Third Reich provides a case study in how governments devise policies and institutions which trespass on just about every human yearning there is, and the human suffering which inevitably follows from those trespasses. It is wrong to detain, torture, and murder humans because they possess an inherent inclination to roam the world freely, to avoid pain, and to preserve their lives. Compulsory sterilization is wrong because humans possess a yearning to reproduce. Proscription of free speech is wrong because it violates the natural human urge to express oneself and communicate ideas to others. Confiscation of property is wrong because humans endeavor to produce things which enrich their lives or can be traded for other things which do so. Requiring accountability or imposing surveillance is wrong because humans desire privacy; i.e., to be left alone. When government interferes with the natural order of things, whether as innocently as planting corn in Siberia, or as atrociously as exterminating persons, there are always disastrous consequences. And even if flouting the natural law benefits a majority (as is typically the claim), there will always be someone who pays the price of having his human nature transgressed upon. Proponents of Positivism and the welfare state have not been able to demonstrate even one credible example to the contrary.

Natural Rights

Natural Rights is a related but separate concept to the Natural Law. If each of us lived on an island by ourselves, we could live without fear of the Natural Law being transgressed. However, almost all of us live in complex societies where social interaction is the norm. The problem is that humans have a frightening tendency to impede the natural inclinations of other human beings, presenting a dilemma: Although humans must be able to mesh with one another, they need to do so in a manner which preserves the Natural Law. Therefore, there is a need for rights which establish rules respecting those interactions so as to reinforce the pursuit of our yearnings implicit in nature. Professor Randy Barnett defines them in the following manner:

> Natural rights attempts to identify conceptually the space within which vulnerable people need to be free to make their own choices about the directions of their lives, which includes crucially the choices of how to acquire, use, and dispose of scarce physical resources.[3]

In other words, our natural rights protect our ability to pursue our natural inclinations free from government interference: To live, to love, to acquire property, to be productive, to be left alone. If a human or if a government transgresses those rights, then it is violating those rules of social interaction, and hence the Natural Law.

Stated simply, because natural rights protect our human nature and are based on the eternal law, they are described as self-evident and inalienable. By self-evident, it is meant that these rights do not require some scientific proof in order to explain their existence. Humans have a natural inclination to preserve their own lives: Although we can certainly try to understand precisely why it is that humans try to preserve their lives, it can stand by itself and needs no further explanation or rationalization. Although a legislature may order that the right to life will be disregarded, it can never take that right away or alter the fundamental human yearning to live, just as Khrushchev could never change the fact that corn cannot grow in Siberia.

Natural rights are in contrast to political rights, which we do in fact acquire by virtue of the government. Thus, in addition to natural rights, we can possess whichever political rights the government guarantees. For example, most of the rights recognized in the Constitution are Natural Rights. However, some, such as the right to be indicted by a grand jury before prosecution, depend upon the Constitution, and not the Natural Law, for their existence. Is there a fundamental human yearning to compel government prosecutors to present a case to a grand jury, at which no judge or defense counsel is present, and the make-up of which is usually timid souls eager to please the prosecutors? Certainly not. Although it may sometimes work as a matter of policy as a check on the government, it has nothing to do with human inclinations and the Natural Law. Nonetheless, it is an additional right which we enjoy by virtue of being under the jurisdiction of the federal government (as opposed to simply being human). Therefore, unlike Natural Rights which can be called pre-political, there are indeed political rights which rely upon government for their existence, and cannot be considered self-evident.

By inalienable it is meant that these rights cannot be taken away from us under any circumstances, although we can give them up. Thus, even if we desired to do so, we could never sell ourselves into slavery and relinquish all claims on liberty. Such a transaction would be void as contrary to the Natural Law. But one may argue, can't we sell our property, thus making it alienable? Although we can alienate our property, we can never alienate our *right* to acquire, possess, alter, and trade property. Thus when we exchange one good for another, we are merely converting the subject of that right into something else; we are not adversely affecting the right itself. If we grew corn and donated it to a local charity, the fact of that donation does not change that we always have a right to claim future corn production for ourselves.

The cornerstone of a libertarian understanding of Natural Rights, and how social interactions should be structured so as to maximize the pursuit of our fundamental human yearnings, is the nonaggression principle. This states that we are free to do as we choose, but only to the extent that our actions do not infringe upon the freedoms of others. Thus, my freedom to swing my arms ends a few inches in front of your nose. In addition to individuals, governments must also obey the nonaggression principle, as governments are merely the constructs of individuals, deriving their just powers from what the governed have consensually given them, and are thus temporal "things" secondary to the Natural Law.

In modern society, where the natural law has been perverted, we have permitted the government to monopolize violence and coercion. This has resulted in our sheep-like acceptance of theft of property, liberty, and dignity by the government. We have also permitted the perversion of the principle of subsidiarity. Subsidiarity encompasses von Mises' assertion that government is the negation of liberty, Aquinas's view that the government's use of force should be as little as possible, and Jefferson's mantra that that government is best which governs least. To comply with the doctrine of subsidiarity, governmental tasks should be performed by the lowest level of government possible, so as to disturb the least individual freedom, absorb the fewest public resources, and endure for the briefest time period. I know what you are probably thinking. . . . This doesn't sound like anything in American government today. You're right.

Elsewhere in this book, we explore a number of different natural rights which embody the nonaggression principle, such as the right to free speech and the right to property. However, whenever we attempt to discuss Natural Rights, the same "problem" that we encountered with the Natural Law arises: What exactly are those rights? As noted above, those who criticize the philosophy of Natural Rights typically do so because they are frustrated by what they perceive to be an inherent subjectivity in the method of identifying those rights. After all, the law prides itself on being objective and determinable. And sadly, the ambiguity of the Natural Law has been abused from time to time so as to disparage our natural rights.

Such was the case in Justice Joseph P. Bradley's concurrence in *Bradwell v. Illinois*, an 1873 Supreme Court case that upheld Illinois' refusal to license a woman as a lawyer. He famously stated that "the constitution of the family organization, which is founded in the divine ordinance, as well as in the nature of things, indicates the domestic sphere as that which properly belongs to the domain and functions of womanhood." Just as geography was once plagued by the belief that the world is flat, so, too, has the practice of discerning the Natural Law fallen victim to ignorance, stereotyping, and invidious discrimination by the government.

The problem with this criticism is that it entirely misconceives the character of natural rights. Rather than be turned off by any sort of perceived subjectivity of determining our "proper ends," we should be instilled with a sense of deep respect for and complete deference to those immutable yearnings implicit in the order of things. It is no more sensible to reject the natural law for its lack of objectivity than to disparage the field of physics for the cryptic behavior of subatomic particles, and thus revert to the belief that all things are made up of earth, wind, water, and fire because it is easier to understand. Subjectivity has absolutely nothing to do with truth, merely the ease and certainty of determining what those truths are.

Our politicians should be terrified at the prospect of encroaching upon our natural rights, and thus interfering with the natural order of things, especially because of their subjectivity, just as we would be terrified to take some experimental medicine about which nothing was known. And as we shall see, even someone who does not believe in the philosophy of the natural law must accept that, if properly followed, it avoids all of the crimes against humanity which we have seen government commit throughout human history. I speak not just of the truth of Natural Rights, but their capacity to foil tyranny.

However, the concept of rights does not in reality have to be complicated at all. Rather, all rights, and indeed all tenets of libertarian philosophy, can be traced back to one single right: The right to own property. Although we traditionally think of this as the right to control tangible, external things (and that is the understanding adopted by the chapter in this book on property rights), it really begins earlier, with a property right to one's own body. If we acknowledge this application of the right in conjunction with the nonaggression principle, then we also recognize free speech, freedom of association, freedom of travel, and a right to privacy. As Murray Rothbard explains in his book *The Ethics of Liberty*,

> A person does not have a "right to freedom of speech"; what he *does* have is the right to hire a hall and address the people who enter the premises. He does not have a "right to freedom of the press"; what he *does* have is the right to write or publish a pamphlet, and to sell that pamphlet to those who are willing to buy it (or to give it away to those who are willing to accept it). Thus, what he has in each of these cases is property rights, including the right of free contract and transfer which form a part of such rights of ownership. There is no extra "right of free speech" or free press beyond the property rights that a person may have in any given case.[4]

If we, however, extend this property right beyond the body and acknowledge that humans must retain control over tangible things external to them, then we also recognize the ability of one to do business and freely contract with others. Moreover, it declares government initiatives such as taxation and the Federal Reserve's inflationary policies as illegitimate and in contravention of the Natural Law. And, as we shall see, some government initiatives, such as war, violate this property right in nearly every single form it can take. Thus, although one may fairly say that libertarians share general principles such as nonaggression and "free markets," among others, the common denominator within this philosophical movement is simply that there are certain spheres of this world which belong exclusively to the individual. We have dominion over these spheres by virtue of being human, and for that reason, they are natural rights which do not rest on any government for their existence.

Human Law

The key difference between the Eternal Law, the Natural Law, Natural Rights, and Human Law, is that the last of these is not implicit in the order of things, but is actually promulgated by humans. Nonetheless, if lawmakers are to create the best society, they must be informed by human nature. Professor Barnett notes the role that man-made law plays in the scheme of Natural Law:

> Once these [natural] rights are identified, it is a somewhat, but not entirely, separate matter of institutional design to see how they can best be protected in a world in which others are more than willing, if given half a chance, to interfere with the well-being of others. . . . Natural rights, therefore, do not enforce themselves. They are rather a mode of normative analysis used to evaluate and critique the positive law that is needed to reinforce them.[5]

The proper role, then, for human law is to extend those natural rights into workable legal standards. After all, we live in an extraordinarily complex world, and it is not always obvious how natural rights, such as the right to order one's personal life, apply to new and controversial questions, such as euthanasia or net neutrality. Moreover, although there may be a natural right to enter into contracts on one's own terms, there is an important role for laws which require that contracts take a certain form before they can be enforced (so as to minimize the possibility of fraud). Although one may intuit that the right to enter into contracts protects the ability of parties to enter into contracts without their signatures, legislatures are well justified in promulgating a law that such agreements will not be enforced. Thus, we can see that man-made law must not only respect, but preserve, protect, defend, and actually serve our Natural Rights.

Because human suffering results when man-made laws conflict with the Natural Law, and the very purpose of man-made law is to enforce Natural Rights, human laws are only valid to the extent that they uphold the Natural Law. Aquinas noted that "every human law has just so much of the nature of law, as it is derived from the law of nature. But if in any point it deflects from the law of nature, it is no longer a law but a perversion of law."[6] As we shall discuss below, one Supreme Court justice even saw fit to distinguish between *acts* and *laws*: Acts are commands which come from our politicians, and cannot be considered laws unless they comport with the Natural Law.

One might well question what is meant by *valid*. After all, we will most likely obey a law regardless of whether it comports with the natural law, so long as the consequence of disobeying that law is punishment. By imposing a requirement of validity, we ensure that our government is constrained by the Natural Law. Could our politicians, practically speaking, pass laws which violate the Constitution? Of course, as is frequently the case. But central to the Natural Law and to the Constitution itself is the belief, held by the people and our judges, that such laws are not valid and should be struck down. So, too, the Natural Law, like the Constitution, will only constrain our government if there are those among us who hold it accountable to the Natural Law.

If there is any message that I hope to communicate in this book, it is that all of us should be constantly questioning the validity of our officials' commands. If they violate the Natural Law, then we must do everything in our power to right their wrongs and restore our freedom; at the simplest, it will entail voting them out of office; at the most extreme, it will mean abolishing that government altogether.

The importance of questioning the validity of Human Law can be seen in the American civil rights movement. Racially discriminatory laws were, of course, often obeyed, because the consequences of not doing so was imprisonment and police brutality. However, civil rights activists, including the Reverend Dr. Martin Luther King Jr., knew that those laws did not comport with the Natural Law, and thus if African Americans were ever truly to be free, they must do everything in their power to have those laws repealed:

> When the architects of our republic wrote the magnificent words of the Constitution and the Declaration of Independence, they were signing a promissory note to which every American was to fall heir. This note was a promise that all men, yes, black men as well as white men, would be guaranteed the *unalienable* rights of life, liberty, and the pursuit of happiness. . . . Instead of honoring this *sacred obligation*, America has given the Negro people a bad check, a check which has come back marked "insufficient funds." But we refuse to believe that the bank of justice is bankrupt. . . . I have a dream that one day this nation will rise up and live out the true meaning of its creed: *"We shall hold these truths to be self-evident: that all men are created equal."*[7]

Dr. King recognized that those laws were not just bad or unwise, but *illegitimate* because they violated the fundamental truths of the Natural Law. Civil rights were not mere political rights which could be granted or taken away as government saw fit; rather, since they come from our humanity, they relied upon nothing from the government for their existence. As we shall now explore, and as noted by Dr. King, this scheme of Natural Law was adopted by our Founders and enshrined in the Declaration of Independence and the Constitution.

The Promise of Freedom

Although our rights would exist even if they were not recognized by the Constitution, a scheme of Natural Rights nonetheless is enshrined in the Declaration of Independence and Constitution, and forms the basis for our entire legal system (or what our Founders intended to be our legal system). As previously noted, Jefferson specifically characterized our rights to life, liberty, and the pursuit of happiness as inalienable and self-evident. Moreover, he justified the entire American Revolutionary War as an effort to restore the protection of our Natural Rights:

> When in the Course of human Events, it becomes necessary for one People to dissolve the Political Bands which have connected them with another, and to assume among the Powers of the Earth, the separate and equal Station to which the Laws of Nature and of Nature's God entitle them, a decent Respect to the Opinions of Mankind requires that they should declare the causes which impel them to the Separation.[8]

Thus, the entire basis for our independence as a nation is the recognition and protection of our Natural Rights. The Founders did not believe that the tyranny of King George III was merely imprudent or unwise but, like Dr. King, found it to be illegitimate.

In 1798, Justice Samuel Chase acknowledged the idea that government behaviors contrary to the Natural Law are invalid when he proclaimed in the famous Supreme Court case of *Calder v. Bull*, which addressed the applicability to state legislatures of the Constitution's prohibition of *ex post facto* laws, that

> there are certain vital principles in our free Republican governments, which will determine and over-rule an apparent and flagrant abuse of legislative power. . . . An ACT of the Legislature (for I cannot call it a law) contrary to the great first principles of the social compact, cannot be considered a rightful exercise of legislative authority.

Thus, government is always constrained in principle by the Natural Law—which Justice Chase called "the great first principles of the social compact."

Natural rights are also referenced in and protected by the Constitution. The Ninth Amendment states that "the enumeration in the Constitution of certain rights shall not be construed to deny or disparage others retained by the people." What would constitute the "rights . . . retained by the people," if not Natural Rights? By proclaiming that those rights are retained, the text of the Constitution expressly rejects the philosophy of Positivism: Because those unenumerated rights remain with individual human beings, Congress and the president cannot take them away by enacting a law or issuing a command to that effect.

Moreover, since the Bill of Rights constrains the federal government, the Fourteenth Amendment protects individuals from similar encroachments of our Natural Rights by the States: "No State shall make or enforce any law which shall abridge the privileges or immunities of citizens of the United States." What would be the privileges or immunities of American citizens, if not our Natural Rights? After all, the amendment does not say, "The enumerated rights in the Bill of Rights shall apply to the States." Thus, states are constrained by more than just those rights expressly listed in the Constitution, but also by those natural rights which are not easily identified and listed. We explore a method for enforcing those rights elsewhere in the book in the chapter called "When the Devil Turns Round on You: The Right to Fairness from the Government." Why the Fourteenth Amendment refers to privileges and immunities instead of rights is an interesting story, but it is of no semantic significance.

Dr. King, in his "I Have a Dream" speech, referred to the protection of Natural Rights as the promise made by our Founders to the American people. Proponents of Positivism must coherently argue why we should now uproot the entire basis for our independence and default on that promise. As we shall now see, they have not been able to make the argument coherently, but they have profoundly uprooted the basis of our independence with their material assaults on the Natural Law.

Positivism

Positivism teaches that law is whatever is affirmatively put forward by human lawmakers. To a Positivist, the law is whatever the lawgiver/lawmaker says it is. Consequentially, under Positivism all of our rights are granted to us by the government, and they can be taken away at the discretion of the government. The central feature of Positivism is that an act is considered a law simply if it was lawfully enacted and is enforceable. In other words, laws are those commands which people can be coerced into obeying. Thus, Positivists would contend that Hitler's Final Solution, regardless of its morality, can be described as law. By contrast, Positivists expressly disclaim that there is any "higher law" with which human law must conform if it is to be truly considered a law. As discussed earlier, Positivism can be a very tempting legal philosophy, given that if government systematically disparages our rights, then as a practical matter it appears as if we do not in fact possess those rights. It is also tempting because, in a free society, whether a democracy or a republic, the majority in the government, the majority of those who write the law, have their way with no constraints. "The majority rules" is a popular, populist, and Positivistic taunt. It is also destructive of freedom.

Why did Positivism develop as a legal philosophy? After all, legal philosophies typically arise in response to a particular situation, just as Natural Law developed during a period of Absolutism, when it was believed that kings were divine, and thus they and their commands were superior to their subjects; during such times of tyranny, the inherent truth of the Natural Law is at its most obvious. Professor Barnett notes that we can literally see the truth of the Natural Law by observing the direction in which refugees travel—toward freedom, and away from oppression.

Positivism is said to accomplish two objectives; the first is that law is "written," and thus, persons do not have to worry about being surprised by unwritten legal obligations binding upon them. Positivists fear that judges who simply disagree with the collective judgment of the people may strike such laws down under the auspices of the Natural Law. If we are to err to any side, it should be the collective knowledge and experience of we the people, not judges. It is for this second reason, as we have seen, that Positivism is described as fundamentally majoritarian. Stated differently, no matter how ill-advised, unnatural, or immoral; how unlawful, unconstitutional, or hateful; how biased, self-serving, or fraudulent; under Positivism, the majority that lawfully controls the government lawfully gets its way. This is the second objective of Positivism.

There are, however, some problems with Positivism, several of which have already been discussed. First, Natural Law thinkers also recognize a need for written, man-made law which can provide guidance and a sense of certainty to the populace. They only pose the additional requirement that those written laws be grounded in the principles of the Natural Law.

Second, Positivism's emphasis on majoritarianism has proven itself to be a woefully inadequate substitute for a scheme of Natural Rights. Although the theory of Positivism allows for the promulgation of laws which favor the majority, it also facilitates the promulgation of laws which benefit a minority at the expense of the majority, as was the case for centuries with Feudalism. Thus, Positivism is contingent upon effectively functioning democratic processes; without them, Positivism collapses in on itself. Anyone discontented with lobbying practices in Washington can understand this flaw of Positivism.

Why should the transgression of the natural rights of a minority be any less abject than doing so to a majority? After all, Jews were an ethnic minority in Germany; does that make the Holocaust any more tolerable? Because the Natural Law applies equally to individuals and minorities as well as majorities, *any* transgression of it is just as damaging to the immutable order of the universe. If we steal one hundred dollars instead of one million dollars, it is still theft, and a violation of another individual's property rights.

As human history teaches us, many of the most egregious human rights violations have come at the hands of majorities in so-called advanced societies. Was it not a majority of white Americans which for two hundred years institutionalized slavery, the ultimate violation of Natural Rights? Even Abraham Lincoln, the so-called Great Emancipator, was not an abolitionist out of principle, but rather out of temporary military necessity to cripple the southern economy and win the Civil War. Was it not democratically elected officials who detained (Asian) Japanese American citizens during World War II, but not (Caucasian) German American citizens? Perhaps the most extreme example of the tyranny of the majority is abortion: Unborn fetuses obviously cannot partake in the political process, and therefore are, for the purposes of this discussion, a minority which has been "outvoted." What could constitute more natural yearnings than to be born and to develop into a human being?! Nonetheless, abortion is a widely accepted practice even in those advanced societies with the greatest protections for fundamental rights.

The requirement that law is whatever can be enforced is also imprudent, and simply untrue. In his speech to the people of London, the character V in *V for Vendetta* eloquently addressed the issues of truth and enforceability in the law:

> There are of course those who do not want us to speak. I suspect even now, orders are being shouted into telephones, and men with guns will soon be on their way. Why? Because while the truncheon may be used in lieu of conversation, words will always retain their power. Words offer the means to meaning, and for those who will listen, the enunciation of truth. And the truth is, there is something terribly wrong with this country, isn't there? Cruelty and injustice, intolerance and oppression.[9]

V, like our Founders and Dr. Martin Luther King Jr., recognized that the truncheon was simply not an adequate substitute for the principles of "fairness, justice, and freedom"; the enforceability of unjust laws cannot change the truth that our Natural Rights are being transgressed.

Conclusion

Although we have explored at length how man-made law must be subject to the Natural Law, perhaps the best indication of the falsehood of Positivism is that, deep down, we *know* that the transgression of our natural rights is wrong. We do not simply disagree with it, but feel a sense of visceral outrage that one human would try to treat us as inferior and subject to his will; it is antithetical to our selfhood. Thus it is in our human nature not just to yearn for freedom, but to recognize when those yearnings are unnaturally restricted.

Elsewhere, V referenced Thomas Jefferson when he stated that "people should not be afraid of their governments. Governments should be afraid of their people." It should be clear that Positivism's scheme of law relies upon the people obeying laws because they are afraid of the government, not because those laws are in accord with the Natural Law, and therefore just.

If we are to live forever in a legal system founded on Positivism, then we can only hope that we will have laws which, coincidentally, happen to be just. But there is another way, the way of the Natural Law: Rather than be content to follow the will of the truncheon, we can choose to listen to those words which enunciate truth, and our Founders' promise that those truths will not be denied by government.

This book is about the titanic battle between adherents of Positivism and believers in the Natural Law; stated differently, between Big Government and individuals. As we shall see, the danger that befalls individuals inevitably comes from the government. The government makes it dangerous for us to be right when it is wrong.

Chapter 1

Jefferson's Masterpiece:

The Declaration of Independence

When I think about current mainstream sentiment, that the federal government can regulate all personal behavior, right and wrong, protect us from every catastrophe, take care of us from cradle to grave, and tax any activity, I wonder: When did Americans lose their way? How have we as Americans strayed so far away from the ideals which brought about the American Revolution? Do most Americans even know that the American Revolution was not the war for independence but instead the *cause* of the war for independence?

John Adams explained in a letter to H. Niles in 1818 when he wrote, "But what do we mean by the American Revolution? Do we mean the American war? The Revolution was effected before the war commenced. The Revolution was in the minds and hearts of the people; a change in their religious sentiments of their duties and obligations."

What were these duties and obligations that changed in people?

The Revolution before the Revolution

What exactly was this Revolution that occurred in people's minds, who started it, and when? Many people consider the British philosopher John Locke to be the grandfather of the American Revolution. Locke was the father of what was formerly called Liberalism; he was one of the most important Enlightenment thinkers, and in 1689 he published his two most influential essays entitled *The Two Treatises of Government*. The second of these two treatises was *An Essay Concerning the True Original, Extent, and End of Civil Government*.

The Freest Nation in the World: The United State of Nature

In his second treatise, Locke traces the evolution of man from when he is born in a state of nature, to being part of an organized society governed by the laws of nature. Locke starts off his theory with a description of the state of nature; where all men are born equal, free, in possession of certain natural rights, and governed by the natural law of morality. This theory of equality means no one has rights that are superior to any others', and these natural rights are rights that are possessed by all people, given by our Creator, as a consequence of our humanity.

Societies will form naturally because individuals will come together in an attempt to acquire various goods and property, which will inevitably lead to conflict because of man's fallible nature. It is for this reason alone that governments will form, with their only roles being the protection and preservation of every individual's natural rights, and the only way the government gains this power is through the consent of the individuals involved. According to Locke, if governments abuse their powers, or if individuals do not consent to their governance, it is the right of the people to revoke their consent or to alter or abolish the government. What is the role of government today? Did anyone actually consent to this government? Where and how do you go about giving your consent, do they even ask for it, is it assumed that you implicitly consent, and more importantly, how do you revoke that implied consent?

Two Wrongs Don't Make a Right

As we can see, our liberties, rights, and freedoms existed before governments are formed, or as French lawyer Frédéric Bastiat stated in 1850, "Life, liberty, and property do not exist because men have made laws. On the contrary, it was the fact that life, liberty, and property existed beforehand that caused men to make laws in the first place." This is a far cry from the mainstream view of rights and liberties in America today; but wasn't Locke's theory the foundational theory upon which America was created in the first place? It seems modern American thought has replaced the theory that the only just role of government is to protect our natural rights, with a theory that the role of government is to give us our rights. How can the government give us what it does not have? What path has this led us down? Does the individual have the right to live his own life as he wishes anymore? It actually seems that some tyrannical central government has assumed this role for him, all supposedly in the best interests of the general welfare, of course.

You Cannot Purchase Rights from Wal-Mart!

It is very important to understand what a right is, especially since Big Government progressives in both the Democratic and the Republican Parties have been trying to trick us. These folks, who really want the government to care for us from cradle to grave, have been promoting the idea that some goods are rights. In promoting that false premise, they have succeeded in moving the debate from *whether* the feds should micro-manage our lives to *how* the feds should micro-manage our lives. This is a false premise, and we should reject it.

What is a right? A right is a gift from God that extends from our humanity. Thinkers from St. Augustine to St. Thomas Aquinas, from St. Thomas More to Thomas Jefferson, from the Reverend Dr. Martin Luther King Jr. to Pope John Paul II to Justice Clarence Thomas, have all argued that our rights are a natural part of our humanity. We own our bodies; thus, we own the gifts that emanate from our bodies. So, our right to life, our right to develop our personalities, our right to think as we wish, to say what we think, to publish what we say, our right to worship or not worship, our right to travel, to defend ourselves, to use our own property as we see fit, our right to due process—fairness—from the government, and our right to be left alone, are all rights that stem from our humanity.

These are natural rights that we are born with. The government doesn't give them to us, and the government doesn't pay for them, and the government can't take them away, unless a jury finds that we have violated someone else's rights.

John Locke advanced our understanding of Natural Rights with his theory which explained what humans were naturally able to do in the perfectly free state of nature. In this state, humans were free to order their own actions, exercise their free will, employ their own person, and acquire and dispose of their own possessions. The state of nature (human existence without government and without the need for government) was also a state of equality; where no one's rights were subordinate to any others' rights. Thus, no person has the right to tell another person how to order his life, and no human may impose his will forcibly or coercively to deprive another human of his free will.

More generally, a right involves a sphere within which we are free to make our own decisions without any interference from the government, individuals, or entities. Just as we gain personal property when we mix our labor with nature to allocate food to ourselves, we then gain the right to be the sole decider of what to do with that property. From this it follows we should also be the sole decider of what to do with all of the other emanations from our bodies. If government were to regulate any of our rights, we would lose our personhood. Rights ensure such a result will not happen.

What is a good? Locke also spoke of humans as animals who naturally need to acquire property. Goods are those "things" we want or need as humans. In a sense, a good is the opposite of a right. Similarly, we have a right to acquire these goods in order to be able to fulfill our wants and needs, at least to the extent that these goods are scarce (unlike air, except for a scuba diver, who then must possess exclusive rights to his oxygen tank). The easiest good to analyze is food because it is such a basic necessity for all human beings. Prior to being claimed by any person on earth, a piece of fruit is no one's property. If fruit is the property of all humans on earth, and could never be privately owned, then every time we bite into an apple, we would be eating someone else's property; or if it is no one's property, then we would be stealing each time we bite. It is unreasonable to believe in a theory that results in humans violating another's rights every time they wish to eat; this would lead to the choice between constant violations of others' rights or starvation.

Nor is the scheme of natural rights a uniquely religious concept. The only premise one need accept is that humans are created; it is immaterial whether it is by God or by nature. If a Catholic scholar declares that the female birth cycle is a miracle from God, and an atheist scientist explains the process with a focus on human biology, anatomy, chemistry, and physics, does it undermine the occurrence of human pregnancy? Of course not; they are just two explanations of the same naturally occurring phenomenon, and though they start off with differing premises, they end up in the same place. Why then should a Catholic scholar's interpretation of Natural Rights being a gift from God be any different from an atheist scientist believing our Natural Rights come from our humanity? Just as pregnancy exists no matter how it is explained, the different explanations of the source of Natural Rights, God or rational humanity, do not change humans' possession of Natural Rights upon our entering into existence.

Governments Protect and Serve Others; You Don't

It is worth noting that the Founders, having experienced the tyranny of both kings and democratically elected majorities, adamantly rejected the notion that rights came from a society, rather than by virtue of being human. But how is such a notion possible? Is society not just a collection of individuals? How could you have the right to liberty, yet at the same time be forced to serve others' best interests? It is impossible, and best explained by Ayn Rand: "It only stands to reason that where there's sacrifice, there's someone collecting the sacrificial offerings. Where there's service, there is someone being served. The man who speaks to you of sacrifice is speaking of slaves and masters, and intends to be the master."[1]

The word *collectivist* is appropriate for this view not only because it is a collective view of society, but also because it is the guardians who are the ones that are collecting our sacrifices, which in their view, we have no right to. No one's rights to life or liberty or property are protected in this system, because if your life and your liberty and your property are not in the best interest of society, then society can take them away, or as the American lawyer, newspaper editor, and politician Gideon J. Tucker said, "No man's life, liberty, or property are safe while the legislature is in session."[2] This is a purely subjective theory of morality; and since any behavior can be rationalized while using a subjective theory of morals, it is a horrible theory upon which to base the governing of a society. Take the southern states in this country in the pre–Civil War era; when viewed as a collective society, dominated by white southern male farmers, was slavery not in the best interest of those who dominated that society? Any theory of government where slavery could be justified is immoral and abhorrent. While slavery might be in the best interest of the majority of members in society, it is definitely not in the best interest of the minorities in that society (the slaves).

History is full of examples of atrocities perpetrated by societies acting under the will of the majority. People tend to forget that Adolph Hitler was democratically elected, but people will never forget what resulted from his reign over Germany. In the antebellum American South, slavery was also present in a democratic society. The majority of voters in the South were white people who were property owners. These people authorized themselves by law to own black people as slaves. The *Los Angeles Times*, in a 1992 editorial about California politics at the time, stated,

> Democracy is not freedom. Democracy is two wolves and a lamb voting on what to eat for lunch. Freedom comes from the recognition of certain rights which may not be taken, not even by a 99% vote. Those rights are spelled out in the Bill of Rights and in our California Constitution. Voters and politicians alike would do well to take a look at the rights we each hold, which must never be chipped away by the whim of the majority.[3]

Amen.

Liberty never lasts in a system where all laws are created by a majority vote; as Benjamin Franklin said, "When the people find that they can vote themselves money, that will herald the end of the republic." It was for this reason the United States was not founded as a democracy. James Madison expressed this view in *Federalist* No. 10 of *The Federalist Papers*:

Hence it is that such democracies have ever been spectacles of turbulence and contention; have ever been found incompatible with personal security or the rights of property; and have in general been as short in their lives as they have been violent in their deaths. Theoretic politicians, who have patronized this species of government, have erroneously supposed that by reducing mankind to a perfect equality in their political rights, they would, at the same time, be perfectly equalized and assimilated in their possessions, their opinions, and their passions.[4]

Our Duty to Protect Our Rights with a Locke

After John Locke created the seeds of Revolution, it fell to someone in America to plant these seeds in the minds of his brethren in order to form a better society. Thomas Paine, a student of the Enlightenment, assumed this responsibility when he wrote and published a pamphlet entitled *Common Sense* on January 10th 1776. It was an instant success. At its time it was the best-selling book in American history, selling about five hundred thousand copies in its first year. This book was so popular because it was a beautiful argument premised on Locke's revolutionary ideas, with the aim of solving the colonists' woes. His solution, of course, was American independence from Britain and the creation of a new and just form of limited governance.

Paine began *Common Sense* by restating Locke's theory of man in the state of nature and why governments are formed. Paine understood his first goal was convincing Americans to go to war with Britain to win independence. To achieve this goal, Paine presented, and refuted, all of the arguments against maintaining the status quo and remaining loyal to Britain.

I Pledge Allegiance, to the Crown, of the United States of America

First, he tackled the theory espoused by British loyalists that since America had flourished under British rule, it should maintain its tight political bonds to Britain. Paine declared this just as absurd as concluding that because a baby had grown by drinking milk, it should never mature to eat meat. Paine even refuted the premise of this argument completely, and instead suggested that America had flourished *despite* British rule over the colonies and not as a *result* of British rule over the colonies.

This debate is eerily similar to a debate between American conservative political commentator Pat Buchanan and Thomas DiLorenzo, an economics professor at Loyola University Maryland.[5] Buchanan suggested that it was because of the institution of central banking and protective tariffs that the American economy saw the greatest progress in world history, progressing from half the size of the British economy in the mid-nineteenth century into twice the size of the British economy in the early twentieth century. DiLorenzo correctly refuted this claim by stating that it was not only despite these government institutions and interventions that the American economy progressed, but that these interventions hindered progress by creating four stock market crashes, and several other boom-and-bust cycles. It is a shame that it is Buchanan's, and not DiLorenzo's, views that are accepted in the mainstream today. Sadly it seems that in the long run, the American Revolution did not change Americans' loyalty to the throne of England; it only replaced the throne of England with the federal government of the United States of America.

That Is Absurd to Me Because I Have Lost My *Common Sense*

Paine then addressed the next argument, which was that Britain's army and navy provided necessary protection to the American colonies. But the protection of the American colonies was for Britain's own financial gain and nothing more. In addition, Paine pointed out that since the colonies were dependent on British rule, they were seen as allies with Britain, and thus forced to be enemies with Britain's enemies. However, if they were independent, then they would no longer be enemies with nations such as France and Spain, with which they had no quarrel.

Why Doesn't the Earth Revolve Around the Moon?

Paine then explained that if the colonies were to reconcile with the British government, the abuses of the present condition would only repeat themselves, which would make it impossible to return to a state of tranquility. Paine called it absurd to believe that Britain possessed adequate ability to govern such a large and intricate land, and we can see this when he wrote,

> Small islands not capable of protecting themselves, are the proper objects for kingdoms to take under their care; but there is something very absurd, in supposing a continent to be perpetually governed by an island. In no instance hath nature made the satellite larger than its primary planet, and as England and America, with respect to each other, reverse the common order of nature, it is evident they belong to different systems: England to Europe, America to itself.

This size and population disparity is the crux of Paine's just form of government. The old system had a crown in the nation's capital that ruled over all the subjects of the land. You can imagine a pyramid of power with the king being on top, then the nobles and military right below him, with the common folk, accounting for most of the population, all the way at the bottom. How could one man be expected to create all the laws that were designed to govern the lives of so many people?

Pyramids Are Naturally Upside Down

Paine attempted to flip this pyramid right on its head. The common folk, or every individual, would make up the laws that were to govern their own lives and property. They would then elect representatives who would create laws, in accordance with the laws of nature (natural rights), which governed social interactions between individuals with the only goal of preserving the individual's rights. These representatives would elect a leader of the colony who would enforce the laws, once again in accordance with the Natural Law, regarding inter-colonial matters.

Surely a system with a localization of power, where every individual is in charge of dictating his behavior, based on what is in his rational self-interest makes a lot more sense than having some Congress with a few more than 500 members create the laws for approximately 310 million Americans. Happiness, peace, and liberty clearly cannot be achieved when one institution is making laws for an entire population, especially when the population it is making laws for is 620,000 times larger than the population of the people making the laws. We have seen in America what happens when 500 people are in charge of making the laws of the land; it is those 500 people whose best interest those laws are designed for. It is certainly not your best interest they are legislating for, but their own. Corruption, cronyism, favoritism, corporatism, and despotism are the likely results of a system that is run with this or any type of central authority. Happiness, peace, and liberty are only enjoyed by the central state, and the powerful elites with whom it is partners. Each individual can only experience happiness, peace, and liberty through a system where he is making the personal choices which govern his own life and regulate what he can do with his own property.

The Military Presence Around the Globe Is Too Big Not to Fail

Once Paine finished with his case for why the colonies needed to fight for independence, his next task assessed America's then current ability to gain independence. He started this off by asserting that the contemporary brewing question was not *if* America would separate from Britain, but *when*. There was no better time than the present (1776), he argued, because at that time America had more than sufficient manpower to form a powerful army, and plenty of resources that could raise a navy, which could be used to defeat the British. Paine affirmed that not only should the colonists create a strong navy for the purpose of fighting a war for independence against Britain, but in addition as a result of Britain's navy being spread thin around the globe during this time in history, Britain was unable adequately to defend the coast of the massive continent from the possible threat of a foreign invasion. Paine thus contended that if Britain continued its rule over the continent, its ability to defend America would become severely deteriorated.

America's military is currently spread over 130 countries in the world and has more than 900 permanent military bases. The maintenance of this foreign empire is costing approximately one trillion dollars per year, as well as countless numbers of American and foreign military and civilian lives. Not only does this make America's homeland defense extremely weaker (and, as we have seen before, it actually creates more enemies), it is also making America's economy extremely weaker, and will inevitably lead to a collapse in the U.S. dollar. Will this scenario not bring about a "deteriorated" United States like Paine had worried about in *Common Sense*?

How Special Is Your Interest?

Paine's urgency was his understanding of the long-term effects British mercantilist policies would have on the economy of the colonies. The passage of the Navigation Acts in 1650 permitted the colonists to trade only with Britain, and if they wished to trade with other nations, the goods traded must first be shipped to British ports. Through this system, Britain was able to force the colonies to focus on the production of raw materials, which were shipped to Britain where they were changed into higher-priced manufactured goods that were shipped back and sold to the colonies. This mercantilist system created large and successful business elites in Britain during this period. As explained in the *Library of Economics and Liberty*, "the mercantile system served the interests of merchants and producers such as the British East India Company, whose activities were protected or encouraged by the state." It was Paine's belief that the British government would just parcel out unused land and resources in the colonies to the same British elites, who were the beneficiaries of the British government's mercantilist policies.

Paine believed this land would be used much more productively by the colonists to do such things as pay down their debts and build a better society. What happens when the United States federal government pursues policies that favor and strengthen certain economic elites, and then parcels out lands and resources to these groups? Everyone certainly remembers the disaster that ensued in the summer of 2010 when the U.S. government gave oil giant British Petroleum (BP) the rights to drill into the sea bed on the bottom of the Gulf of Mexico. After the Exxon *Valdez* disaster off Alaska in 1989 had been cleaned up and nearly paid for by Exxon, the oil companies lobbied the Congress for liability limits—maximum amounts that they could be held to pay in the event of a disaster. A Republican Congress and President Clinton together made it the law that oil companies would be limited to pay seventy-five million dollars for cleanups, and the taxpayers—that would be you—would pay the rest. In return, the feds would be able to tell the oil companies where to drill, and how to transport their oil.

In the case of BP, it asked the State of Louisiana if it could drill in five hundred feet of water, and Louisiana said it could. The federal government vetoed that and told BP it could only drill in five thousand feet of water. Never mind that no oil company had ever cleaned up a broken well at that depth and never mind that the feds had never monitored a broken well at that depth and never mind that BP only needed to set aside seventy-five million dollars in case something went wrong. The feds trumped BP's engineers, and the feds trumped the wishes of the folks who live along the Gulf Coast, and the feds decided where this oil well would be drilled.

Disaster struck. The feds did nothing. Oil gushed out in an amount that is so great as to be immeasurable. Political pressure grew. President Obama eventually panicked because he believes that his federal government can right every wrong, regulate every activity, and protect us from every catastrophe ("Daddy, did you plug the hole?"). He is wrong. Louisiana Governor Bobby Jindal was ready to build barriers to protect his State's coastline, and the feds said no. The President even invoked powers that allowed him to supervise the cleanup using BP personnel and equipment. And the oil still gushed. Then, the President stopped all oil drilling in the Gulf, putting thousands out of work.

Then, he demanded billions from BP so his team could decide who gets it, and a terrified BP gave him all the cash he asked for.

So, the government that foolishly limited BP's maximum liability, the government that claimed it knew where best to drill, the government that actually stopped locals from protecting their own shoreline—that would be the same government that bankrupted Social Security, Medicare, Medicaid, the post office, Amtrak, and virtually everything it has managed—now wants to decide who gets BP's cash.

The last time this government had this much private cash to give away, during the GM and Chrysler bankruptcies, it disregarded well-settled law and gave it to the labor unions. To whom will it give this cash—the innocent injured or its political friends?

The government cannot protect us from every catastrophe, especially ones its rules have facilitated. How about this: That government is best which governs least. The people have a right to a government that obeys the laws of economics, the laws of physics, and the Constitution. Let private enterprise do what it does best, and keep politics out of the way. If the Constitution was written to keep the government off the people's backs, it is time for the feds to get off.

I Revoke My Consent to the Government's Declaration of Dependence

Some important and influential American colonists recognized Paine's criticisms, and consequently exercised their positive moral duty to disobey an unjust government, a duty to which we will return in the last chapter of this book. These colonists, who were all delegates of the thirteen colonies, gathered together to form the first Continental Congress of the United States of America. Their first job was to form a committee of delegates to draft the first law of the United States, which was the Declaration of Independence. On June 11th 1776, the Congress appointed Thomas Jefferson, John Adams, Benjamin Franklin, Roger Sherman, and Robert R. Livingston to a committee in charge of drafting the declaration.

Thomas Jefferson's Movin' On Up on the Free Side

This committee then voted to delegate the responsibility of drafting the declaration to Thomas Jefferson and John Adams. John Adams subsequently passed the sole responsibility to Jefferson because of Jefferson's education in the classical liberal philosophy espoused by John Locke on which the Declaration was to be based. Also, Adams gave three other reasons for why Jefferson should draft the document: "Reason first, you are a Virginian, and a Virginian ought to appear at the head of this business. Reason second, I am obnoxious, suspected, and unpopular. You are very much otherwise. Reason third, you can write ten times better than I can."

Most Americans are aware of the existence of the Declaration of Independence, but when was the last time you read it? Or better yet, when was the last time you heard someone quote, speak, or teach about the Declaration of Independence? Many times when I quote this document in conversations I have with many Americans, highly educated people nonetheless, they have not the slightest clue of where the quotes I speak of originate. Some even maintain that it was something written by Karl Marx!

Let us now look at the text of the Declaration of Independence. The most important section is the second paragraph, because it is where all of the meat is found of the colonists' moral and political philosophies on which they were basing the need for independence:

> We hold these Truths to be self-evident, that all Men are created equal, that they are endowed by their Creator with certain unalienable Rights, that among these are Life, Liberty, and the Pursuit of Happiness.[6]

As we have seen, a self-evident truth is a statement of fact that proves itself; one that needs no explanation. As we have also seen, one of those self-evident truths is that all men are created equal. An important distinction must be made here. The meaning of *equal* is not meant to be construed as the equality of ability, brain power, wealth, or that all men are equal in every conceivable sense. However, it restated Locke and Paine's position, which was that no man has a mandate from God to rule over other men. What this moral position sets up is a governmental system or a society where the king, even if his name is George, or Abraham, or George W., is not a superior moral instrument with power over the natural rights of the people whom he attempts to govern.

Put differently, no man is endowed with rights superior to anyone else; and this is the absolute fundamental principle on which Locke and Jefferson wrote and upon which the American government was formed. No scientific study or knowledge should be needed to conclude that it is a self-evident truth that the best system of governance is one that recognizes and guarantees equality of rights for all.

The next part of the Declaration goes on to state "that they are endowed by their Creator with certain unalienable Rights, that among these are Life, Liberty, and the Pursuit of Happiness." In the old days, the king could essentially do no wrong since he was actually regarded as the only person who had the power to create the laws, which power the ancient beliefs held was given to him from God. Since this was the case, then the king was to make all laws and rule all of his subjects, and this was seen as the only means of achieving peace.

When Jefferson recognized the truism that all men are created equal, he was introducing a government in which the rights of every man were recognized and respected by every other man, even those in the government. When Jefferson stated that all humans are endowed with "certain unalienable Rights," he meant that not only are we all born fully possessed of our rights, but these rights are unalienable, meaning they can only be surrendered by conscious intentional criminal behavior. As Jefferson wrote, "Everyone would agree that each of us is born without governmental permission or involvement. It is evident our very lives come from nature or God. The government does not breathe life into anyone." Jefferson certainly was not introducing the system we have today; where Congress gains its powers from a majority vote and then has the ability to right every wrong, and regulate every behavior. Where does a government get its power from? Jefferson answered. That to secure these rights, governments are instituted among men, deriving their just powers from the consent of the governed.

The common usage of the word *secure* has been corrupted over the years to mean "to obtain" as well as "to safeguard." When this line was penned, however, *secure* only meant "to protect," so, just as Locke said men are born with certain rights, to make certain no one can take these rights away from them, men created governments. This sentence also restates the Western premise that governments can only come about, and gain just powers, through a contractual agreement between those who are governed and the government. You must take note that nowhere does Jefferson assert that a government may attain its just powers from the consent of a *majority*. This means that the consent to be governed must be given by every single person, which also means that if any single person does not give his or her consent to the powers the government exercises over him or her, then they may in fact be unjust powers.

Conclusion

Wouldn't it be in every American's best safety and economic interests to bring an end to this madness? The stranglehold the federal government has over our everyday lives is almost impossible to escape without a complete abolition of the government. How has the government been able to gain the powers necessary to grow so large?

Having explored the history and original understanding to the Declaration of Independence, we are now in a position to delve into the Natural Laws which the Declaration sought to secure. And we shall also see that throughout our history, the principles of the Declaration have been trod upon time and time again. If we, as the colonists, continue to live under the yoke of an unjust government, then we must similarly exercise our natural right to disobey the government.

Chapter 2

Get Off My Land:

The Right to Own Property

In 1985, Henry Weinstein bought a commercial building at 752 Pacific Street in Brooklyn, New York. Never in his wildest dreams did he imagine that twenty years later the government would take it away and hand it over to a private developer. Weinstein said he would have been shocked if his property was taken away for a highway, library, hospital, or bridge; however, seeing it taken to pave the way for Forest City Ratner's (FCR) Atlantic Yards project was in his own words "the most un-American thing [he has] ever experienced." FCR, owned by Bruce Ratner and Russian mogul Mikhail Prokhorov, then sold tax-free bonds to finance the development's keystone venture: An 18,000-seat basketball arena for the New Jersey Nets at Flatbush and Atlantic Avenues near downtown Brooklyn. Was America supposed to be a country with a government that can just take away your property against your will and transfer it to a basketball team?

American history is riddled with stories such as this one of the government either physically taking private property or regulating the usage of the property to the extent where it is rendered useless. Many historians believe that a sovereign state has an inherent right to seize private property. This power originated from tyrannical monarchies in Europe. For example, in 1066, William the Conqueror seized practically all of the land in England. While he maintained absolute power over the land, including the right to repossess it, he granted temporary possessions, called *fiefs*, to landholders who served as stewards. In return for this favor, the stewards paid fees, pledged allegiance, and provided military services to the king.

Could you imagine living in a system where you could never own your own property, but instead, you could only possess property while constantly having to pay to use it, and provide your leaders with military service in the event of war? It should not take such a wild imagination to envision this, considering that currently in the United States, we live under such a system. Individuals are forced to pay income taxes for the fruits of their labor. The product of your labor—wages—becomes your property, and when the government taxes it, the government is saying, "We have granted you the right to work. In return you must pay us for the privilege." As well, we are forced to pay property taxes on our land, and if we do not, the land gets seized by local authorities. At least we are not forced to serve in the military, right? *Wrong!* When the military draft was instituted in World Wars I and II, and the Vietnam War, refusal to fight was punishable by a penalty of up to five years in federal prison and a fine of up to $250,000.

In the United States, the power of eminent domain is recognized within the Fifth Amendment's Takings Clause which states, "Nor shall private property be taken for public use without just compensation." Jeffersonians did not believe in granting the government a power of eminent domain. Jefferson, and the soon-to-be anti-Federalists, argued that only by mutual consent, and fair bargain, but never against your will, could the government end up owning your property. Conversely, Alexander Hamilton, and the soon-to-be Federalists, believed the government had an absolute right to take any property it wished, just like the British kings at one time could and did.

James Madison, the great compromiser and principal author of the Constitution, persuaded the delegates to add the Just Compensation Clause. This was a most unfortunate compromise. While it required the government to pay fair compensation for whatever property it takes, and while—on paper—it required that property could only be taken for "public use," it also permitted the government to take whatever it wants. Does the government exist to serve individuals, or are we here to provide for the government's greater wealth?

First a Basketball Team, then a University

Norman Siegel represents Tuck-It-Away Associates (Tuck-It-Away), which is fighting the decision of the Empire State Development Corporation (ESDC) to condemn and seize its land in order to transfer the property to Columbia University, a private entity. Tuck-It-Away is a self-storage business located in the Manhattanville area of Harlem where Columbia University is planning to expand its campus. Since Columbia's plans could make the property more valuable, the ESDC classifies this as a public benefit, which is one of the justifications for eminent domain. Siegel has said, "Basically they are saying if there is a Motel 6 and Hilton comes along and says they can make the property more valuable, then it [the Motel 6] can be declared blighted."[1] Siegel also said that many public advocates have begun saying the land in these cases should not be labeled "blighted," but "coveted."[2]

New York's highest court upheld Columbia's expansion plans, which allowed it to go through with its $6.3 billion expansion project. Tuck-It-Away still has a glimmer of hope, as it has petitioned to the United States Supreme Court. Siegel noted, "This is the first time ever that a private education institution can constitute a civic project," and Nicholas Sprayregen, owner of Tuck-It-Away Inc., said, "It is truly a sad day for anyone who cares about the sanctity of private property rights."[3]

I'm Sorry, but Taking Your Property Will Improve the Economy and Our Campaign Finances

Before the Weinstein and the Tuck-It-Away cases came before a court, one of the most egregious Supreme Court assaults on private property took place. In *Kelo v. City of New London* (2005), the Supreme Court ruled that a group of homeowners could have their property taken from them by the local city council and have it transferred to a private entity. The reasoning was that the new "shopping village" would attract a new corporate headquarters for pharmaceutical giant Pfizer, thus creating many new jobs and added tax revenue, which would in turn benefit the public. The thinking here was that the public is better off having corporate giants take over individual homeowners' land, because they could use the land better than the homeowners could. Must we now be slaves to our own land, making sure that we are using it in the most productive way for the entire community? Shouldn't we be able to use our own land however we see fit?

Justice Sandra Day O'Connor noted this in her dissenting opinion when she said,

> The specter of condemnation hangs over all property. Nothing is to prevent the State from replacing any Motel 6 with a Ritz-Carlton, any home with a shopping mall, or any farm with a factory. . . . Any property may now be taken for the benefit of another private party, but the fallout from this decision will not be random. The beneficiaries are likely to be those citizens with disproportionate influence and power in the political process, including large corporations and development firms. As for the victims, the government now has license to transfer property from those with fewer resources to those with more. The Founders cannot have intended this perverse result. "That alone is a just government," wrote James Madison, "which impartially secures to every man, whatever is his own."

Justice Clarence Thomas sounded a jurisprudential fire alarm in his dissent when he said, "Something has gone seriously awry with this Court's interpretation of the Constitution." And I do not believe he was only speaking about this specific case either. Justice Thomas, clearly the most faithful to the Natural Law of all current sitting justices, also expressed his concern that the Court permitted the government to value its economic interest above the individual homeowner's personal values that are protected by the Natural Law. The Natural Law mandates that the choice of personal values (a book or TV, a bicycle or car, early to bed or up all night) is completely immune from government interference unless the exercise of that choice substantially and unfairly interferes with another's Natural Rights.

In a bitter twist of fate, on November 9th 2009, Pfizer Corp.—the intended beneficiary of the Kelo cottage—announced that it would leave New London in 2011, moving most of its New London employees to nearby Groton, Connecticut. This proves that the New London City Council is not as intelligent as it originally thought. Apparently, Pfizer was allowed to determine what was best for its property, and it determined it was best to get away from its relationship with the New London government. The "urban village" shopping center was never built, and the lot that was seized remains vacant and barren. So now, the City of New London, which seized the Kelo real estate expecting a real estate tax windfall, collects no taxes on the earth where the Kelo cottage once stood. The government thought this piece of land would better serve the community as a vacant lot, rather than remain the homes of its lawful owners.

Government's Just Power

Kelo was a case of seizure by the State of Connecticut. States' appetites for private realty are voracious, and so is the feds'. How can the federal government even make an argument to legitimize any eminent domain power? The Constitution delegated specific powers to the federal government, reserving all other powers to the states, including the police power. Thus, whatever power the federal government has to secure rights is limited to federal territory and is limited to the exercise of one of the federal government's enumerated powers. Any federal effort to regulate private land for the public good must be accomplished under some other enumerated power. Any such effort to regulate would then be constrained by the Just Compensation Clause; if the private property owners are not compensated for the losses they incur by federal regulations, the costs for the "public benefit" of these regulations fall entirely on the private property owner.[4]

Unlike the police power, which is to be restricted to the protection of rights, the eminent domain power is not a just power. A just power is a power possessed by individuals, and delegated in whole or part to the government. No private person would have the right to condemn any of his neighbor's property, no matter how good the intentions. So, if persons lack this power themselves, how could they delegate it to government? And if not delegated to the government, then the government lacks the power.

"We Are the police. Put Down All of Your Weapons and Give Us Your Property."

In 1992, a twenty-two-year-old soldier was driving his Honda in downtown Washington, D.C. He was waved to the curb by a woman. It was actually a male police officer in drag who was over six feet tall, weighed 220 pounds, dressed in a black dress, red wig, and red flats. The cop said the soldier said he was looking for a date. The soldier said that the cop offered him sexual services for twenty dollars, to which he responded, "Yeah, okay," and then he proceeded to drive away. He was later stopped by other police officers and arrested. The police dropped the charge of solicitation of prostitution, for unexplained reasons, but they seized and kept his car, and argued that it was forfeited under a law providing for seizure of vehicles used to solicit prostitution. The "Yeah, okay" (which normal people would interpret as "no way") was enough to establish probable cause that an offense was committed. Probable cause is all that was needed to justify the forfeiture. On the night that a similar law went into effect in D.C., the police seized three cars and a mountain bike. It just so happens that it is general practice for police officers who seize property to take personal ownership of the property, and either keep it for personal use or sell it at public auction; what is being incentivized here is theft under the guise of law. Where are the courts and lawyers that are supposed to be watching out for our rights?

Buyer Beware . . . of the Government

Justice Oliver Wendell Holmes Jr. stated in *Pennsylvania Coal v. Mahon* (1922) that "while property may be regulated to a certain extent, if regulation goes too far it will be recognized as a taking." And the Fifth Amendment requires the government to pay for takings. How far does a regulation have to go to be considered a taking?

In 1996, a small college in Buffalo bought an old rectory. The college planned on tearing the rectory down to make way for a parking lot. Community groups petitioned the City to designate the building as a landmark which would make it untouchable. The preservation board recommended a denial of the petition, but this recommendation was overruled by the Buffalo City Council. The college asked for compensation on the grounds that the City had taken its property. The City refused to pay, and the court upheld the denial based upon the legal fiction that the property was not taken, even if it was now worthless to the college. The local groups now have the benefit of the use of the land without the inconvenience of paying for it, and the college has a worthless building.[5] This is a clear injustice and an outrage.

In 1983, Joan Dawson bought a three-unit brownstone in Harlem. She moved in with her two grown children, two foster children, and a grandchild. Two of the units were renter-occupied and covered by rent control, but the law allowed an owner to take over an apartment for family use. That was precisely what Dawson planned. In 1984, New York City changed its landlord-tenant law so that tenants who lived in an apartment for twenty years could not be evicted under the owner-occupancy rule. Dawson sued, arguing that the change in the law took her property. She lost, and the court arrogantly noted that she should have known better than to rely on existing law since laws can always be changed. In 1994, she had to re-purchase her home by paying the tenants to leave. Apparently, the New York City courts are well aware that property rights, as well as many other rights, can simply be changed at the whim of the legislature. Is this justice?

Leave My Bundle Alone

Naturally, there are certain rights that come with property ownership. These rights are the right to use your property however you see fit; the right to exclude anyone, including the government, from trespassing on your property; and the right to alienate, or transfer, any or all of your property interests. It is very important to understand that the word *property* is not synonymous with *land* or *a house*; your land and your house are types of property. Your money, which is earned by the fruits of your labor, is also your property. As well, and most importantly, your natural rights are your property. Assuming that the government's eminent domain power was legitimate, every time it limited, restricted, or took away any of our rights, it would have to provide us with just compensation. When President Bush signed the Patriot Act into law, taking away our rights to privacy, due process, *habeas corpus*, free speech, and freedom from illegal searches and seizures, did any one of us receive any just compensation for these takings?

If You Want to Use Your Property, You're Going to Have to Run It by Us First

At common law, people were not required to obtain a permit in order to use their property as they wished. Common law limits free use only when a use unfairly invades the property rights of others. The law calls this a nuisance. Tell that to a landowner in Pacific Grove, California, on the Monterey Peninsula. If a landowner there wants to build a house, he or she must get approval of the plans. This approval process requires twenty public hearings and the approval of the Architectural Review Board, the Planning Commission, the City Council, and the California Coastal Commission. The process takes three and a half years and requires more than six hundred thousand dollars for costs, lawyers, and studies. During one hearing, an Architectural Review Board member said, "In my former life as a seagull, I was flying up and down the California coastline and saw your house built shaped as a seashell." She subsequently voted against approving the plans for a non-seashell-shaped house; so much for that common law standard whereby you were not required to get a permit to use and enjoy your property.

This common law rule has been challenged on a more philosophical level with calls for immigration reform. As Glenn Jacobs, the wrestler "Kane," notes, Americans clamor that illegal immigrants are destroying "our" hospitals. However, these hospitals belong solely to their proprietors, not to "us."

We have no ownership rights over them whatsoever, and are wrong to impose reforms that would limit to whom the hospitals' proprietors can provide services. Although immigration policies may accomplish this result in a more back-door, surreptitious manner, it is still just as antithetical to a Natural Law scheme of private property rights as the state seizing them directly.

A New Way to Take Property

University of Chicago Professor Richard Epstein's 1985 book, *Takings: Private Property and the Power of Eminent Domain*, supplied the momentum for a challenge to the regulatory takings. Epstein proposed to challenge the entire New Deal as "inconsistent with the principles of limited government and with the constitutional provisions designed to secure that end."

One of the provisions of the New Deal that Epstein called an unconstitutional taking was minimum wage law. Epstein asserted that minimum wage laws are "undoubted partial takings, with all the earmarks of class legislation, which requires their complete constitutional invalidation." This was the case because employers are forced to pay a statutory minimum wage frequently higher than wages set by the free market. These business owners suffer from a government taking of their property, since they can no longer use their property as intended; because they are forced to spend more of their money, which is their property, on labor.

Epstein also claimed that collective bargaining was "yet another system in which well-defined markets are displaced by complex common pool devices whose overall wealth effects are in all likelihood negative and whose disproportionate impact, especially on established firms, is enormous." Epstein raised the question: Who feels the adverse effects of collective bargaining? He then answered this by stating that adverse affects were felt by the owners of the "established firms." Collective bargaining has increased the economic means of the great majority of working people in the United States by securing decent wages and benefits for union members, and driving wages higher even for the unorganized.[6] But it is involuntary (since the government forces it upon business owners), and therefore it violates the Natural Law and the Constitution by compelling the owner of a business to negotiate with all of his employees as if they were one; thus, it produces higher wages, higher costs, higher prices, and theft of property from the businessperson.

There are many other regulations that violate property rights as well; in fact almost all regulations violate property rights in some way or another. Tariffs, excise taxes, duties, and sales taxes violate the property rights of the sellers of the goods because the price for their goods is raised, making them less competitive and less profitable; as well, the buyers of these goods are forced into paying higher prices for goods, thus parting with more money than would have been the case had these regulations not been in place.

Bundle of Sticks

Not only does property ownership come with a bundle of rights, but each of these rights can be sold or transferred. The owner of a house can transfer his rights of use, possession, and exclusion to a tenant for a defined amount of time, in a lease. An owner can also grant specific uses to another individual via a licensing agreement. Thus, a private agreement, by consent, can restrict use of property. But any governmental regulation that restricts use, possession, or exclusion is an invasion of the property owner's rights, as it makes the property less valuable. Once again the cost of the regulation that is intended for some public good is thrust upon the property owner. These costs do not require just compensation because courts have adopted a 100 percent standard. This standard states that owners are only entitled to compensation where regulations restrict complete usage of their property, or where their property is rendered completely useless.

The Story of General Widgets

If you own a widget-producing factory and the government decides one day that it is going to charge you a widget licensing fee of one hundred thousand dollars per year for the privilege of being allowed to use your land how you wanted to, this not only decreases the value of your factory, since there is a hefty cost imposed on anyone who wishes to use it, but it also is a taking of one hundred thousand dollars of your property every year.

Then, let's say the next year the government decides to pass legislation which requires that all widget producers hire union workers; we will call them the United Widget Workers union or the UWW. Now, to produce widgets you must give workers higher wages, bigger benefit packages, longer vacation times, shorter working hours, and better pensions for retirement. This legislation also forces you to associate with a specific union, giving the union great bargaining power in any collective bargaining agreements in the future, so much bargaining power that you are forced to guarantee that you will never use improved machinery or robots that could produce widgets faster and more efficiently than any of the current union workers because then they would be out of a job. This severely reduces the productive capacity of your factory, which also reduces the value of your business; and it also forces you to pay higher production costs, which is another taking.

To make matters worse, your main widget-producing competitor from Asia has an unregulated widget factory comprised of only robots that are producing the cheapest and highest quality widgets in the world. Now your business is relegated to bankruptcy. And this is precisely when the government will swoop in to bail out your creditors, kick you out of the management office, purchase your business and factory for pennies on the dollar, and transfer ownership of it to your union workers, the UAW. I mean the UWW.

Offer, Acceptance, Consideration . . . and Government Approval

The right to transfer property leads to the right to contract freely. All that is needed for a viable contract is for there to be an offer, an acceptance, and some consideration. For example, I offer to sell you this book for X dollars, and you agree to purchase this book for X dollars; we therefore have a viable contract. My consideration is the amount of money you paid; your consideration is the book you receive. Of course, the government, which has provided no services to either of us in connection with this book sale, forces my publisher to collect a sales tax from you, forces you to pay it, increases the cost of the book beyond the X dollars we agreed upon, and thus takes property from both of us.

There are various other ways governments have interfered with the freedom to contract. People who enter into contracts are dictating the law for themselves; the law would be the terms of the contract. The government is constitutionally restrained from interfering unless there is a breach of contract or the essence of the contract is unlawful. One of the greatest assaults on contracts was in *Home Building & Loan Association v. Blaisdell* (1934). In response to the rise in defaults on mortgages during the Great Depression, Minnesota passed a statute in 1933 which extended the period during which borrowers could reclaim their property from foreclosure by their creditors. The precise question before the Court was whether the law violated the Contracts Clause of the Constitution (Article I, Section 10), which expressly prohibits states from "impairing the Obligation of Contracts"—here, lending agreements. The Court upheld the legislation on the grounds that the Contracts Clause was not intended to be absolute, and consequently a subjective showing of state emergency was sufficient to override the clear text of the Constitution.

While I am no great defender of U.S. banking interests, I am a great defender of the U.S. Constitution, and the constitutionality of legislation is the only thing that should be considered by the Supreme Court. This was precisely the sentiment expressed by Justice George Sutherland, who wrote one of my all-time favorite dissents:

Whether the legislation under review is wise or unwise is a matter with which we have nothing to do. Whether it is likely to work well or work ill presents a question entirely irrelevant to the issue. The only legitimate inquiry we can make is whether it is constitutional. If it is not, its virtues, if it have any, cannot save it; if it is, its faults cannot be invoked to accomplish its destruction. *If the provisions of the Constitution be not upheld when they pinch as well as when they comfort, they may as well be abandoned.* (Emphases added)

This Game Is Called "Was the Building Bombed or Rent Controlled?"

Another way government intervenes in the right to contract freely is through rent control. Originally designed during World War II to provide housing to people of lower income in wartime and protect them from war-related housing shortages, rent control is a government-imposed price ceiling on the amount of money a landlord can charge in rent. Today it still exists, however, and is abused by many people who could afford to pay the real going rate for their rental property. Ed Koch, the cantankerous ex-Mayor of New York City, for example, in the early 1980s paid $441.49 for an apartment then worth about $1,200.00 per month.[7]

In a free market, if the demand for rental apartments is greater than the supply, prices will rise to remove the shortage, by both bringing forth new supply from investors who will seek to take advantage of this new profit opportunity, and by reducing the amount demanded.

When price controls are instituted, a shortage results. First, since the price ceiling is set below the market rate for rent, a shortage in the stock of low-income apartments naturally follows. The demand for rentals is then spilled over to the non-controlled sector, which normally consists of higher-priced apartments. This increase of demand, combined with increased fear by landlords to invest in new property since governments could impose rent control on those apartments as well, causes the rental prices of these non-regulated apartments to skyrocket. So, while prices in the controlled sector might be lower, the overall cost of renting will be much higher than the cost a free market would command.

Second, with the increased uncertainty in the whole market, investors will pull their money out and search for greener pastures. Also, because of this decreased profit incentive, landlords will not reinvest in their properties for such things as ordinary maintenance, thus causing the property to deteriorate over time. This, surprisingly, is something all economists tend to agree on. Socialist economist Assar Lindbeck even stated, "In many cases rent control appears to be the most efficient technique presently known to destroy a city—except for bombing."[8]

Setting the Precedent for Destruction

Where did the federal government get the power to regulate all economic behavior? *Wickard v. Filburn* (1942) was the case that greatly increased the federal government's power to regulate our lives. Roscoe Filburn, an Ohio farmer, produced wheat in excess of the amount allowed by the Agricultural Adjustment Act of 1938. He was not selling the wheat, or bartering with the wheat; he simply grew the wheat, on his own land, for his own personal consumption. Mrs. Filburn ground the wheat into flour and used the flour to bake bread for the Filburn family. The Roosevelt administration, drunk on New Deal socialism, effectively told Mr. Filburn to stop growing so much wheat for his family and told Mrs. Filburn to stop baking bread and cookies for their children. (FDR was in the period of his wretched life during which he was admiring and imitating his dictator friend, "Uncle" Joe Stalin.) There was no commercial activity and no interstate activity taking place with this wheat; so then, how could the federal government restrict the amount of wheat a person grows on his own land, for his own consumption?

The Interstate Commerce Clause in the Constitution was designed to give Congress the power to regulate commerce between foreign nations, states, and with Native American tribes. The original meaning of the word *regulate* was "to keep regular." Its sole purpose was to prevent states from creating tariffs to be used to the detriment of merchants in other states. When the feds sought to fine Filburn for growing and consuming too much wheat, the Supreme Court of the United States ruled that if farmers were allowed to grow any amount of wheat they wished, this in the aggregate would affect the price of wheat, which would affect interstate commerce, thus validating the Congress's power to regulate interstate commerce. Of course, everyone knows that growing and consuming your own wheat that you grew in your backyard is not a commercial activity, takes place in one state, and has *no* measurable effect on interstate commerce. Somewhere Madison is fuming.

Congress has since abused this power to no end. Not only has the government regulated the remedies for defaulting on loans, not only has it regulated the amount of wheat grown in our backyards, it has regulated the number of hours per day bakers can spend turning that wheat into bread, and the wages they can be paid, and the temperatures of their ovens!

The Gift that Keeps on Giving: The Community Reinvestment Act of 1977

The government completely trampled the right to contract freely in the Community Reinvestment Act (CRA) of 1977. It essentially mandates that banks contract with less-than-desirable borrowers in an effort to increase home ownership across the nation. No mutual consent was required; rather, the government coerced private banks to abandon their traditional business practice, all in the name of political gain and extra votes.

During the Carter administration, people accused mortgage lenders of racism because poor urban dwellers who were mostly black were being denied loans, while suburban whites were not. Seeking to reduce "discriminatory" credit practices against low-income neighborhoods (this practice is called *redlining*), Congress took this indictment as a green light to do anything— including interfering with private enterprise—to get more money into the hands of minorities to increase home ownership (this is not the job of the government, by the way).

The Community Reinvestment Act made it legal for the government to twist the arms of private banks to make loans to "less-than-creditworthy borrowers," thereby forcing private banks to associate with clients not of their choosing, but rather of the government's choosing. To hold control over these lenders, Congress empowered a number of regulatory agencies to punish those banks that were not meeting the credit needs of "low-income,

31

minority, and distressed neighborhoods." The government's threat to these lenders was real. Agencies like the Federal Reserve, the Comptroller of the Currency, the Office of Thrift Supervision, and the Federal Deposit Insurance Corporation could examine banking institutions for CRA compliance (or non-compliance) and take this information into consideration when approving applications for new bank branches or for mergers or acquisitions. Banks were bullied into loosening their standards and, as a result, made questionable loans to those who could not afford them.

Generally, banks make loans based on the personal variables of the borrowers, such as the size of the mortgage payment relative to income, credit history, and income verification, for example. But in the wake of the Community Reinvestment Act, the federal government informed banks that participation in "credit-counseling" programs was sufficient as proof of a low-income applicant's ability to make mortgage payments. "Banks and lenders, forget about those other 'silly' factors—you know, like, *the numbers*. Trust us. We are the government."

A credit-counseling program? Seriously? What kind of proof is that!? Per the government's extortion, banks were forced to make loans based on nonexistent credit standards. The quality of loans being handed out by private banks (because the government mandated it) was like candy at Halloween.

Michael Lewis, in his book *The Big Short*, recounts the plight of an immigrant strawberry picker with an annual income of $14,000 who was given a loan for a $700,000 home. In what kind of world is this loan reasonable? The CRA was one of the many ways the government attempted to provide affordable housing to low-income people. Interestingly enough, after this government scheme caused the real estate bubble that wrecked the economy in September 2008, the solution it proposed was to prop up housing prices to extreme heights that were artificially bid up by speculators; in other words, the program designed to provide more affordable housing kicked many homeowners out of their houses, wrecked the economy, and attempted to solve the wreckage by keeping housing prices higher or at more unaffordable levels for poor people. The irony of government actions never ceases to amaze me.

Through the passage of the Community Reinvestment Act of 1977, the government chose to ignore a little fact: Businesses have the right to contract freely with individuals or companies with whom they freely choose to contract. That is their fundamental right.

Recklessness with Contract Rights

Today, with the Chrysler bailout, we see the current establishment's complete recklessness when it comes to the contract rights of Chrysler's bondholders. The bondholders are secured creditors, which means by law they hold a higher ranking than shareholders or unsecured creditors in a reorganization or bankruptcy. Outrageously, though, the government—which has inserted itself into this private bankruptcy by virtue of its massive loans to Chrysler—completely ignored this ancient and uniformly applied rule and instead intimidated a federal bankruptcy court to award ownership shares to the United Auto Workers, and only what was left to the bondholders.

When the bondholders tried to get a larger stake in Chrysler, President Obama publicly referred to them as "vultures," and they eventually backed down. Since when are you a "vulture" just because you ask that the contract you signed be enforced, that the money you loaned out be paid back? And since when does the President interject himself into the fray when a lender wants a loan repaid? When contracts don't mean anything.

The government can be counted upon to interfere with any contractual relationship it hates or fears. Congress has wielded its interstate commerce power to create a federally mandated minimum wage. Minimum wage directly affects the poorest members of the economy, and while this is precisely the intention, the results happen to be completely contrary to these intentions; at least the intentions of the few good-hearted politicians. Many ignorant lawmakers assume that poor people will make more money simply because a law raises the lowest wage an employer can pay a poor person. However, since the poorest members of society tend also to be the least skilled members, if the minimum wage is set above the level of production that a poor person can achieve with his current skill set, then he will never get a job; and the higher the minimum wage, the higher the barrier poor people have to jump in order to gain employment.

If a person's skill set is valued at five dollars an hour by an employer, this valuation will not change just because the government implements an eight-dollar minimum wage. What will happen is this person will not get the job; what employer will hire a worker who will actually generate a negative return? So, instead of a poor person having the opportunity to hone his skill set and learn the valuable lessons of hard work that would make him more employable while raising his value, feeling of accomplishment, and the wage he can command in the future, this poor person is rendered unemployable and forced to live a substandard life on the welfare dole because of government-mandated minimum wages. Since many poor teenagers do not possess adequate access to a decent education (as a result of the terrible public school system as discussed in chapter 11), they will suffer the most.

These teens are at a severe disadvantage when they face competition from middle- and upper-class teenagers who have access to better educational systems and who are also able to present themselves better while on interviews. The main weapon a poor inner-city teenager would have in this situation would be the willingness to work for a lower wage; this way he could increase his chances of successfully competing against the middle- and upper-class teens for employment by giving prospective employers a cost-saving incentive. Once he gained employment, he could learn useful skills, demonstrate his true worth to the employer, learn how a certain business works, build a resume, and command a higher wage in the future. However, since government restricts the ability of an individual to choose how much his own labor is worth, he is forced to remain unemployed, never getting an opportunity to learn very important working skills. This is all, of course, supposedly in the greatest interest of the general welfare.

Conclusion

The Interstate Commerce Clause has become an extremely formidable weapon, one which Congress uses to assault our individual commercial liberties and steal our property every day. If Congress is allowed to use this power to regulate food that we grow in our own backyards and consume in our kitchens, there is no limit to its power. Every behavior can now be taxed and regulated by the federal government, and this is something that must be stopped. We have seen examples of how government restrictions and takings have destroyed houses, apartment complexes, businesses, as well as the entire American economy. We have seen how these same restrictions on private property made housing unaffordable for the poor and the middle class; we have seen restrictions cause extreme poverty amongst the most marginalized members of society. When will this end?

It is no wonder the American economy is no longer the strongest economy, with the most productive and innovative people in the world. America, just like Europe at the end of the two great world wars, has been left with limited factors of production and a ravaged economy. But, unlike Europe, America was not a casualty of war, and our factories were not bombed by enemy tanks and aircraft; Americans have had their productive capital taxed away, their costs of living increased, their education diminished, and their factories have been allowed to rust, become outdated, and waste away, all thanks to onerous government taxes and regulation; all thanks to government's lack of respect for the inalienable right to own private property.

Chapter 3

Names Will Never Hurt Me:

The Freedom of Speech

Approximately 1,160 miles separate Topeka, Kansas, from Westminster, Maryland. Fred Phelps, pastor of the Westboro Baptist Church in Topeka, Kansas, feels it is his duty to travel great distances to spread his congregation's religious message: "That God's promise of love and heaven for those who obey him in this life is counterbalanced by God's wrath and hell for those who do not obey him." In 2006, this duty brought him to Westminster, Maryland, to attend a funeral service at St. John's Roman Catholic Church.

The funeral was in honor of Lance Corporal Matthew Snyder, a U.S. Marine who died while stationed in Iraq. Funerals such as Corporal Snyder's are prime opportunities for Phelps to spread his religious message, because he believes God is punishing the United States for "the sin of homosexuality" through a multitude of events, including soldiers' deaths likes Snyder's. However, Phelps's protests do not end with him or his followers attending funeral services. They attend the funeral services while shouting at grieving family members and carrying signs with slogans such as, "Thank God for Dead Soldiers," "Priests Rape Boys," and "God Blew Up the Troops."

Is this form of speech the exercise of a natural right granted to us by virtue of being human? Is there a fundamental yearning to communicate ideas to others, even if those ideas are patently offensive and outrageous? More importantly, *should* it be? After all, legal Positivists might criticize any scheme of rights, such as the Natural Law, which protects the protesting activities of Fred Phelps. As we shall see, however, freedom of speech is a nearly absolute right which can only be curtailed in the direst of situations, namely, where speech will somehow infringe upon other natural rights, as might be the case with a criminal mastermind instructing his henchmen to kill others. As unpopular as Fred Phelps's ideas might be, we cannot, and must not, conflate questions of unpopularity and offensiveness with natural rights. If we do, then we set a legal precedent for the suppression of unpopular groups, and the death of free thinking. As Noam Chomsky stated, "If we don't believe in freedom of expression for people we despise, we don't believe in it at all."

"They Chose Liberty"

The egregious and loathsome speech of Fred Phelps is a prime example of the speech the First Amendment protects. In drafting the First Amendment, the Founding Fathers intended to protect not only agreeable or non-provocative speech, but also speech against the status quo. Indeed, the American Revolutionary movement was itself an uprising against then existing power structures, making its literature the object of government contempt. Justice William O. Douglas wrote, "The framers of the Constitution knew human nature as well as we do. They too had lived in dangerous days; they too knew the suffocating influence of orthodoxy and standardized thought. They weighed the compulsions for restrained speech and thought against the abuses of liberty. They chose liberty."[1]

By choosing liberty, the Founders sought to protect our most basic yearnings: Here, the yearning to think as we wish, and to communicate thoughts to others without the "chilling" effects of government regulation. To avoid repeating history and suffering the later abuses of a tyrannical government, the Founders, in enacting the First Amendment, secured our right to dissent, to speak out against those in power, and to participate in a public discourse. Thus, the right protects not only the speech itself, but every person's ability to express ideas. If others do not agree with those ideas, then they are free to disregard them wholly. They may only seek government infringement of speech if it is somehow violating their own natural rights. No society could exist if there was a natural right not to be offended.

The First Amendment states in part, "Congress shall make no law . . . abridging the freedom of speech." Singularly, this line recognizes the natural right to free expression and restrains the Congress from interfering with that right. It also acknowledges the fact that the right to free speech is a natural or fundamental right. That the Founders wrote *"the* freedom of speech" makes it clear that they viewed the right as pre-existing the government's formation. Thus, the government can only curtail your right to free speech when you violate the Natural Law; otherwise, it has no authority to do so, and any regulation of the right is an illegitimate exercise of power. It should also be clear that the freedom to speak, unlike the freedom to swing one's arms or shoot a gun, will be by its very nature almost never able to harm another. The possible window where speech can violate another's natural rights, and thus be eligible for government regulation, is extraordinarily narrow.

Interestingly, because the Founders believed free speech to be a natural right, they were not always in agreement as to whether it should be inserted into the Constitution. Some argued the Constitution was only a granting of limited power to the federal government by the states, so there was no need to proclaim what rights the states and people retained. After all, where in Article I is Congress authorized to regulate speech? If there was no *explicit* grant of a power to curtail a right, then there would be no need to recognize that right in the document. Madison initially shared this view. He believed the Bill of Rights was not necessary because the rights in question "were reserved by the manner in which the federal powers are granted." Moreover, he had previously experienced the inefficiency of a bill of rights on multiple occasions within state governments;[2] an enumeration of rights could prove extraordinarily dangerous, since the inclusion of only some rights could lead some to believe that other rights do not exist.

Moreover, freedom of speech is in accord not only with original understanding, but the political theory of good governance. The theoretical justifications for freedom of speech can be divided into three categories. First, freedom of speech is necessary to foster a marketplace of ideas. For every thousand brilliant ideas, there are a million exchanges of nonsense. How is truth weeded out? It is not by the government, or even a democratic majority for that matter, arbitrarily determining the truth for itself. No, it is by allowing those ideas to be exchanged, debated, and nurtured. Only this process, and time, will reveal truth.

Second, and related to the marketplace of ideas, freedom of speech is necessary to have an effective government because voters must have access to information in order to make well-informed decisions. If the government could restrict certain individuals' freedom of speech, namely, political opposition, then voters would be unlikely to recognize the flaws in the status quo or discuss better alternatives. Indeed, such is the very purpose of this book. And after all, if there is such a thing as popular sovereignty, how could the employers (voters) properly "instruct" their employees (government workers) if they did not have the ability to speak?

Finally, and as mentioned earlier, freedom of speech is at the core of our individuality. Although the above justifications might shield political speech, artistic and musical expressions are clearly just as deserving of protection. Does one need a message to convey in order to enjoy singing in the shower and writing poetry in the comfort of one's own home? Clearly not. As Justice Thurgood Marshall once said, "The First Amendment serves not only the needs of the polity but also those of the human spirit—a spirit that demands self-expression."

As stated previously, the primary intent of the First Amendment was to secure the Founders' and their peers' right to dissenting opinions, particularly opinions in the realm of politics. Without free speech, there would be no free market for ideas and the exchange of political ideals. Where would our nation be if those who objected to proposals at the Constitutional Convention or the state ratification conventions were carted off to jail? Our country would not be the great nation it is today without the ability to speak freely about our representatives and those in power. A society where speech is restrained is not a free society at all; it is a dictatorship.

Attempts to limit the freedom to dissent are sadly as recurrent as they are damaging to liberty, and America is no exception. History reveals that our right to free speech often ebbs and flows with the temperature of the nation. Too often in times of war Americans are willing to sacrifice their natural rights and allow their passion and fears to override their sensibilities. A wave of fear often envelops the nation, and Americans begin to equate dissent with disloyalty to our country. When these "opportunities" present themselves, the government will often attempt to restrict our natural right to free speech through prohibitions against so-called incendiary or dangerous speech. Unfortunately, the government's primary objective in enacting these restrictions is so often to quell political dissent and unrest.

One need look no further than at the same individuals who drafted the First Amendment to find the first curtailment of our natural right to free speech. Following the French Revolution, President John Adams signed the Alien and Sedition Acts of 1798, with the stated purpose of protecting America from enemy powers (at the time, the government of France) and stopping seditious persons from weakening the new government. The most contentious Act was the Sedition Act, signed into law on July 14th 1798, which made it a crime to publish "false, scandalous, and malicious writing" against the government or most of its officials. As the Alien and Sedition Acts show, no government, not even one comprised of the Founders who sought to safeguard our natural rights, can be trusted to permit robust freedom of speech. How could members of the same generation, indeed in some instances the same persons, who wrote, "Congress shall make no law . . . abridging the freedom of speech," enact a law that abridged it?

More than a hundred years later, Americans experienced another setback to their First Amendment rights. By June 15th 1917, the United States entered World War I. President Wilson, labeling it the "war to end all wars," proposed, and Congress enacted, the Espionage Act of 1917. Title I, Section 3, of the Act made it a crime for any person, during wartime, (1) willfully "to make or convey false reports or false statements with intent to interfere with the operation or success of the military or naval forces of the United States or to promote the success of its enemies"; (2) willfully to "cause or attempt to cause insubordination, disloyalty, mutiny, refusal of duty in the military or naval forces of the United States"; or (3) willfully to "obstruct the recruiting or enlistment service of the United States." Violators of the Act faced fines up to ten thousand dollars, imprisonment of up to twenty years, or both.

Under the Espionage Act, roughly two thousand Americans were prosecuted for opposing America's involvement in World War I.[3] Among these prosecutions was the case of Charles T. Schenck, who at the time was an official in the U.S. Socialist Party. Schenck was prosecuted and convicted for conspiring to violate Section 3 of the Act when he supervised the distribution of leaflets likening the draft to slavery and calling involuntary conscription a crime against humanity. Moreover, he urged those subject to the draft not to "submit to intimidation," and to exercise their right to oppose it. In other words, Schenck was merely exercising his personal sovereignty over the government: It is the government which is the servant of the people, and the people should be free to instruct others on what actions the servant should take. What right does the servant have to punish his master for giving him certain orders?

The Supreme Court unanimously upheld his conviction.[4] Justice Oliver Wendell Holmes, Jr., declared that the relevant inquiry for incendiary speech should be whether the speech creates a "clear and present danger that . . . will bring about the substantive evils that Congress has a right to prevent." Under this reasoning, Holmes believed speech or written materials, which may be appropriate during peacetime, may pose a clear and present danger to military goals during wartime. Moreover, under this test, an individual's conviction may be based on the potential to cause a clear and present danger, regardless of whether this was the individual's intent. How can one be thrown in jail because he said something that had an impact on others which he did not even intend? Justice Holmes was correct; there was very much a clear and present danger: It was the opinion of the Supreme Court.

On the same day as the *Schenck* decision, the Supreme Court upheld two other convictions under the Espionage Act.[5] In the case of *Frohwerk v. United States* (1919), the Supreme Court unanimously held that a "conspiracy to obstruct recruiting would be criminal even if no means were agreed upon specifically by which to accomplish the intent. It is enough if the parties agreed to set to work for that common purpose." Essentially, persuasive words alone could constitute a conspiracy in violation of the Espionage Act.[6] In other words, the object of government regulation crept from physical actions and into the direction of mere thought and speech.

Frohwerk received ten years in jail for writing a series of editorials. In fact, Frohwerk wrote for a German-language newspaper in Missouri. How many Americans in 1917 were able to read and speak German? How many Americans were reading newspapers from Missouri? And while this newspaper did not have a wide audience, even if it had been *The Wall Street Journal*, the First Amendment protects speech questioning the government's decisions, for without this speech the government becomes a despot as to which no one can question any decision.

The common theme in these cases is that government, whether it be the legislative, executive, or judicial branch, has regularly suppressed the speech of political opposition, so long as it could produce an argument that the speech might cause harm.

Consider in this regard the following case. In 1917, Robert Goldstein produced a film entitled *The Spirit of '76*, which portrayed the Wyoming Valley Massacre. During the Massacre, British soldiers abused and killed women and children. While the events portrayed occurred almost 150 years before the production of the film, Goldstein received a sentence of ten years in prison because the government convinced a federal judge and jury that Goldstein's factual account of the Revolutionary War could promote mutiny in the military because it showed our once adversary and then ally, Great Britain, in a "negative" light.[7] The government saw fit to prosecute an individual for accurately portraying events occurring 150 years before the production of the portrayal. Put another way, the government punished an individual for accurately depicting history. Where does it end? If every textbook publisher maintained the risk of heading to jail for publishing darker periods in our nation's history, how would our textbooks read?

Justice Holmes, who wrote *Schenck* and *Frohwerk*, revealed himself to be the ultimate legal Positivist. He asserted that law is man-made, and thus, the government could restrict rights whenever it wished. The Founders anticipated these arguments, and drafted the First Amendment to prevent just such a result: They wrote "Congress *shall make no law*" abridging the freedom of speech, not "may at times abridge" the freedom of speech.

Despite the Supreme Court's earlier deference to the unconstitutional actions of the legislature and executive, in 1969 it did an about-face and began to move toward the proper protection of speech as nearly absolute. Clarence Brandenburg, an Ohio Ku Klux Klan leader, invited a Cincinnati reporter to cover a Klan rally in Hamilton County, Ohio. The events filmed by the reporter show several men in robes and hoods with firearms while burning a cross and making a speech. The speech included reference to the possibility of taking "revengeance" against "niggers," "Jews," and those who supported them.[8] Brandenburg called for a march in Washington, D.C., on July 4th 1964, and was subsequently arrested under Ohio's criminal syndicalism statute. The Ohio statute, enacted during the Red Scare in 1919, intended to punish those who advocate "crime, sabotage, violence, or unlawful methods of terrorism as a means of accomplishing industrial or political reform."

Brandenburg received a one-thousand-dollar fine and ten years in prison. He appealed his conviction all the way to the Supreme Court, which issued a monumental decision. The Court found the Ohio statute to be unconstitutional because it punished "mere advocacy" of unlawful action. According to the Court, and what is still current law, the United States Constitution does not allow the federal government or state governments to proscribe mere advocacy of the use of force or unlawful action, "except where such advocacy is directed to inciting or producing *imminent* lawless action *and* is likely to incite or produce such action."[9] Neither the federal government nor the state governments can pass laws to silence offensive or inflammatory statements that are not likely to result in imminent lawless action, or in other words, violations of natural rights. All innocuous speech, the Court declared, is absolutely protected. And all speech is innocuous when there is time for more speech to resist it.

Free Speech in Political Elections?

Despite the merit of *Brandenburg*, the battle over freedom of speech has raged forward. Today, the factual nature of the cases is significantly different than *Brandenburg* or *Schenck*, but as any natural rights advocate can recognize, the principles are the same. We know that individuals have a natural right to free speech, and only through due process can this right be stripped. But what about groups of individuals who choose to express themselves collectively?

Take, for example, the publicly condemned holding in *Citizens United v. Federal Election Commission* (2010). The Supreme Court invalidated a sixty-two-year-old statute prohibiting corporations and labor unions from utilizing general treasury funds to support or defeat a candidate in the sixty days preceding an election. The majority opinion, written by Justice Anthony M. Kennedy, held that the First Amendment does not allow for the government to distinguish between speakers in order to determine who can voice their support for political candidates. As Justice Kennedy wrote, the First Amendment "has its fullest and most urgent application to speech uttered during a campaign for political office." Moreover, the fact that one speaker may have more wealth than another does not necessitate a ban on speech.[10] Bill Gates most likely has more money than you and I combined, but a ban on his speech simply on account of his wealth would be patently unconstitutional.

As this book is being written, political opposition to *Citizens United* is mounting, threatening to undo its progress. Opponents of the decision claim there will be corruption in the electoral process, as individuals' opinions will be overshadowed by corporate prerogatives, and the holding will lead to a future in which the President is chosen by the Board of Directors of General Motors. (Ironically, it is far more likely today that the President will choose the Board of Directors of General Motors than the other way round. But that is for a later chapter.) However, while these dire predictions might be worth debating, it is the corporations' and unions' constitutional right to endorse the candidates of their choosing. After all, our Founders did not seek to found the most convenient or efficient form of government, but the government which would best guarantee our fundamental liberties. Critics of *Citizens United* err in their failure to recognize this point.

The Obscenity of Obscenity Restrictions

Just as there are vehement critics of *Citizens United* and its protection of groups of individuals, there are also many who seek to regulate speech which they find to be "obscene." *Miller v. California* (1973) involved an individual who conducted a mass-mailing campaign to promote his business selling illustrated books with adult pornographic material. In trying to define what speech is "obscene" the Court developed a three-part test, which is still used today: Works or speech are obscene if (1) the average person, applying contemporary community standards, would find the work, as a whole, appeals to the prurient interest, (2) the work depicts or describes, in a patently offensive way, sexual conduct specifically defined by the applicable state law, and (3) the work, taken as a whole, lacks serious artistic, literary, political, or scientific value.

This standard is riddled with problems. First, it is a blatant violation of the Natural Law to restrict speech merely on account of its offensive nature. It presumes that government may assault natural rights, and that presumption indicates that we exist to serve the government. Are freedoms subject to the government's whims really freedoms at all? As stated before, there can be no natural right not to be offended. Moreover, one can simply avert one's eyes and ears if he is truly offended. *Miller* itself demonstrates the hypocrisy of such a doctrine: The recipients of Miller's mailings did not have to open them up and view their contents; they could have just thrown them in the trash and successfully avoided any offense. If, however, they *voluntarily* view the pictures inside of a mailing which clearly contains pornography, they cannot later claim that they were offended, and thus seek the protection of the law. By insinuating that people cannot stand on their own two feet without the aid of the government, such a doctrine is demeaning to both the individual who is deprived of his natural rights, and the individual who is "offended."

Moreover, such a doctrine is hopelessly subjective, and thus offers arbitrary protection of our natural rights. How can judges determine what is of artistic, literary, political, or scientific value? Not even experts in art, literature, politics, and science are able to do so! Surely, Darwin's contemporaries did not believe that his theory of evolution was of any scientific value; where would science be today if his ideas could have been suppressed merely because they were unpopular? Moreover, it is clearly in violation of the Natural Law to judge speech according to community standards; the Natural Law transcends temporal local cultures. Similarly, the Constitution does not grant the government the power to restrict your speech based on moral or value judgments, nor does it grant the government the power to criminalize speech, which is legal in some parts of the country and illegal in other parts. The Constitution and the Natural Law are universal. The whole purpose of the First Amendment is to assure that individuals—and not the government—choose what to think, say, publish, hear, or observe.

Not Now, Not There, and Not Like That

It should be clear by now that the government does not view the First Amendment as protecting speech it fears, hates, or finds offensive. However, the government additionally attempts to regulate where and how you enjoy your natural right to free speech through so-called time, place, and manner restrictions. To illustrate this type of restriction, consider the act of burning an American flag to show your discontent with public policy. Clearly, the government would despise the content of such expression, and seek to restrict it by any means. However, the government might also choose to regulate your ability to burn an American flag by prohibiting you from doing so in an area where fires are banned. Thus, the government is restricting the *place* in which you can express yourself, rather than the permissible content of your expression. It is that former type of restriction to which we now turn our attention.

Although time, place, and manner restrictions may seem less severe than content-based restrictions, nonetheless they should not give the government any more license to regulate speech. It still must demonstrate that the restriction on expression is necessary to prevent the violation of another's natural rights. Let us consider a few examples. If you lived in a very crowded area, would the government be justified in preventing you from blaring extraordinarily loud music at midnight, or at least requiring you to pay "damages" to your neighbors for doing so? Certainly, by playing obnoxious music, you are diminishing your neighbors' natural right to the use and enjoyment of their property. And over time, if you were habitually noisy, then most likely you would decrease the market value of their property. Thus, although the government could not *criminalize* this kind of expression, it would be more than justified in making it actionable, or in other words, the basis for a lawsuit.

But what about restrictions on picketers outside of your house, and not on your property? Assuming you could enter and leave your house just fine and they weren't being so noisy as to diminish the use and enjoyment of your property, then there would be absolutely no justification for any restriction of their freedom of speech. In what way are your natural rights violated? Although it might be embarrassing, there is no natural right to be free from embarrassment. Does it seem as if they are invading your privacy? Then simply close the blinds. In sum, although it may seem inconvenient and annoying, the protesters' fundamental liberty to express themselves must prevail.

I was shocked during a trip to see the Redwoods at the Muir Woods in Northern California to find a small, government-mandated "First Amendment Zone" located adjacent to a parking lot and hundreds of yards away from the Redwoods. How effective can environmental speech activists be when they can't get anywhere near the trees they want to protect? What gives the government the right to restrict our speech like this on our federal park lands?

Where Do We Go from Here?

While the last few decades provided for the removal of many governmental restrictions on our natural right to free speech, it appears as though the War on Terror may halt these best efforts. As we have seen, so often it is fear of insecurity which provides the impetus for restrictions on speech. Under the Patriot Act, for example, the FBI is provided with the authority to write National Security Letters, or in other words, self-written subpoenas and warrants. Moreover, if an FBI agent shows up at your door with a self-written search warrant, the agent may command you not to tell anyone else about the search—not your spouse at home, your priest in a confessional, your doctor, or your lawyer; not even in a courtroom, *under oath*, without violating the Patriot Act and risking a five-year sentence in prison.

Furthermore, the Supreme Court recently held that a section of the United States Code dealing with terrorism is constitutional, even though it makes it a crime "knowingly [to] provide material support or resources to a foreign terrorist or organization."[11] Material support or resources refer to "any property, tangible or intangible, or service, including currency or monetary instruments or financial securities, financial services, lodging, training, *expert advice* or assistance," a near total ban on not just support to a foreign terrorist or organization, *but interaction with.* Thus, if you were to encounter an individual identified as a foreign terrorist and attempt to encourage him to read the Constitution and understand the vast amount of freedoms we enjoy in this country, you could be prosecuted and convicted for providing "advice." Even more frightening is that the secretary of the treasury and the secretary of state are empowered to classify or declassify any group as terrorists at any time. We simply cannot allow our freedoms to be eroded; not in the best of times, and not in the worst of times.

Conclusion

The most frightening aspect of recent restrictions on speech is not the loss of our ability to speak, publish, and hear what we wish, but the fact that these are mere symptoms of a fundamental flaw in American political culture: We no longer believe that the government exists to serve our needs as individuals and members of a community, but that the government is our master which is able to determine for itself what is in our best interest, unbound by any constraints. No one seriously believes that granting the government the ability to hack into our e-mail accounts (as the Patriot Act does) is truly in pursuit of American liberty. However, what people *do* believe is that there is nothing fundamentally illegal or unnatural or unconstitutional about granting government such a blank check: Although these policies may be "misguided," folks today believe they are not in contravention of the Natural Law *per se.*

With such a view, we are one tenuous showing of necessity away from becoming complacent with such illegitimate commands, as occurred with the Iraq

War (few seriously challenged the lawfulness of the war, but merely whether it was militarily necessary). What is needed is not merely greater accountability, propriety, or guidance on Capitol Hill, but a seismic shift in the way Americans think about the constitutionally mandated role—and contours—of government. Anything less will accelerate our eventual path to serfdom.

Chapter 4

I Left My Rights in San Francisco:

The Freedom of Association

The notion of a gym being sued for declining to hire a fat aerobics instructor sounds more like a South Park episode than reality.[1] However, Jennifer Portnick—a 5-foot 8-inch, 240-pound woman—has gone and done it. Ms. Portnick applied to become an aerobics instructor at Jazzercise, a private gym in San Francisco that markets itself as "the world's leading dance-fitness program."[2] Jazzercise chose not to hire her, citing its company policy: Instructors must have a "fit appearance."[3]

Ms. Portnick took her case to the San Francisco Human Rights Commission, which enforces the City's ordinances, basing her argument on hyper-sensitive San Francisco's "fat and short" ordinance; the law forbids employers from discriminating on the basis of height or weight. In the end, the Commission enforced San Francisco's anti-discrimination law in favor of Ms. Portnick, and as a consequence, the government *forced* the gym to hire the 5-foot 8-inch, 240-pound woman as its newest aerobics instructor at Jazzercise.[4]

Does the government own Jazzercise? Does the government work in Jazzercise's HR department? Of course not; the state is grossly overstepping its authority here. The government does not have the right to tell Jazzercise who it can and cannot hire. The government does not have the right to intrude on a private business owner's right to run his business as he pleases. The government does not have the right to dictate to Jazzercise what is (and what is not) good business practice. All these decisions are *solely* the interests of the business owner and his or her team of advisors.

This ridiculous San Francisco illustration aptly demonstrates how the government, without restraint, continues to violate the fundamental rights of free individuals and private business. In the case of Jazzercise, the state completely obliterates a private business's fundamental freedom of association.

Freedom to Associate Also Means Freedom *Not* to Associate

The First Amendment of the United States Constitution guarantees the freedom of association. It states, "Congress shall make no law . . . abridging . . . the right of the people peaceably to assemble."[5] Simply stated, we may voluntarily gather, come together, or assemble ourselves into whatever peaceful associations we choose, and the government cannot interfere with those choices. It is worth noting that this fundamental right is worded such that it restricts government action; it does not restrict our action. As we have seen, the authors of the Constitution and the Bill of Rights believed that individuals have certain natural rights as human beings, and the government was created to protect these rights, not to violate them.

However, just because the Constitution says that we can associate with any individual we please does not mean that we may associate with any individual we please. The freedom to associate is predicated on the existence of mutual consent—each person must agree to associate with the other person. For example, when A and B agree to associate with one another, both A and B have that freedom. But if A wants to associate with B, and B does not wish to associate with A but is *required* to do so, then B is not legally free to reject that association with A. Rather, he is being *forced* to associate with A. This concept is called *forced association*. Forced association is completely counter to our natural rights as free individuals because it infringes upon a person's right of free choice, and it is counter to the Constitution.

As a result, the right to associate has two components. Firstly, we are free to associate with those who accept us. This is called *positive freedom of association*.

Secondly, we are free to abstain from associations of which we do not approve. This is called *negative freedom of association*. Both elements of the right are integral to the freedom as a whole, both are natural rights, and both are protected by the First Amendment to the Constitution.

Because forced association is inherently not voluntary, it is a form of involuntary servitude strictly prohibited by the Thirteenth Amendment of the Constitution which states, "Neither slavery nor involuntary servitude, except as a punishment for crime whereof the party shall have been duly convicted, shall exist within the United States, or any place subject to their jurisdiction." No involuntary servitude shall exist, and it is the government's job to prevent it.

This tendency to assemble and unite with other human beings is as natural a tendency as they come. There is an internal and innate yearning to be a part of a group with a purpose, a similarity, or sometimes even a distinction. So long as the association does not cause harm to others—"an intentional physical invasion or aggression of another person's body or rights or property"—we have every right to associate with those who want to associate with us. This fundamental right is at the very heart of liberty because it is an extension of the liberty of conscience and freedom of travel. The government must have no role outside of protecting that freedom.[6] The rationale behind the theory is simple. Thomas Paine explains,

> In those associations which men promiscuously form for the purpose of trade or of any concern, in which government is totally out of the question, and in which they act merely on the principles of society, we see how *naturally* the various parties unite; and this shows, by comparison, that governments, so far from always being the cause or means of order, are often the destruction of it.[7]

Where It Gets Sticky in Our Hyper-sensitive, PC World: The Right of the *Individual* and *Private Business* to Discriminate

From the very beginning, we must make a distinction between private and public entities. The rights of a private business are identical to those of an individual because a private business is a compilation of free individuals. This concept is founded on property principles and freedom.

These private entities—both individuals and private business—have the fundamental right to associate, and alternatively, the right not to associate. Conversely, public entities—like the government—do not have this natural right because the state is a fundamentally different kind of unit (which I will discuss shortly within this chapter).

Free individuals have the right to choose the people with whom they associate. The corollary of that right is free persons can choose the people with whom they do not associate. And to take it a step further, the right *not* to associate with others is synonymous with the right to discriminate against others. Because we are free individuals with mental capabilities and decision-making skills, these choices to associate and discriminate are ours, and the government must not interfere. In fact, the government exists to protect this right to discriminate.

While the right to discriminate may sound wrong or even immoral, this is not the case at all. Every day, we make discriminating decisions that result in an exclusion of some kind. When I invite a small group of friends to my home, some of my larger group of friends are included, and some are not. When I have a pizza delivered, I choose one restaurant and eliminate the other options. When I hire a new staff member, I hire one person and reject the other applicants. When I board the subway, I choose to sit in the seat next to one person over a seat next to another person. When we say that a person has "discriminating taste," it signifies a good quality—that she has sophisticated style.

If we did not have the right to make these discriminating choices (which always result in some kind of exclusion), we would be the victims of force or coercion. Walter E. Williams, a professor of economics at George Mason University, further illustrates this concept and right in his article, "The Right to Discriminate":

> Should people have the right to discriminate by race, sex, religion and other attributes? In a free society, I say yes. . . . When I was selecting a marriage partner, I systematically discriminated against white women, Asian women and women of other ethnicities that I found less preferable. . . . The Ku Klux Klan discriminates

against having Catholic and Jewish members. The NFL discriminates against hiring female quarterbacks. The NAACP National Board of Directors, at least according to the photo on their Web page, has no white members.[8]

There is nothing wrong with these discriminating choices at all. Professor Williams and each of these organizations have every right to exclude people and make discriminatory decisions because they fall into one of the following three categories: Free individuals, private groups, or private companies. Not one is a public entity; therefore, they are all free to associate and to discriminate.

Regrettably, with all the benefits that come with this fundamental right to associate, there are also unfortunate consequences. People make good associational choices, but people also make bad associational choices. But the truism here is: Freedom entails the right to make bad decisions. As a result, as morally repellant as it may be, a racist has the legal right to be a racist. A misogynist has the legal right to be a misogynist. A homophobe has the legal right to be a homophobe. And while the existence of these kinds of people in the world is disappointing and aggravating, they have every right to discriminate based upon their prejudices because they are free human beings. The government is here to protect free choices—even bad ones—from the tyranny of the majority.

Why There Really Is No Difference

If Mrs. Murphy decides to host a garden party in her backyard, she is free to invite her fellow Irish friends over to enjoy her fresh-squeezed lemonade. At the same time, she may also (intentionally or unintentionally) exclude her Italian neighbors because she owns her house and has the right to be the gatekeeper of its front door. She may discriminate between invitees because Mrs. Murphy has the absolute right to decide with whom she associates in her own home. Few would dispute this fact.

If Mrs. Murphy sets up a lemonade stand outside her home on her property, she is free to serve only those customers she wishes. She may refuse to sell her lemonade to the Muslim family down the street. While this is a bit harder to swallow than the previous example, it is *her* lemonade to sell, *her* property to sell on, and *her* choice to make poor business decisions, which exclude a portion of her lemonade-buying population. Because Mrs. Murphy has the right to decide with whom she associates, she may discriminate between potential lemonade-buyers.

Lastly, if Mrs. Murphy opens up a pub down the street, she may still choose to serve only those she wishes to serve. There is really no difference between this scenario and the lemonade stand situation; the food and service are hers to sell, the pub is her property, and it is her choice to make poor business decisions to exclude customers. As a private business owner, she has that freedom because the government has no business telling Mrs. Murphy how to run her private company, the pub. It is not, however, in Mrs. Murphy's interest to deny her Italian, Muslim, or black neighbors entry because she will lose business, the business of those excluded and the business of those that abhor Mrs. Murphy's racism.

Laurence M. Vance, an adjunct scholar of the Mises Institute, equates the private home scenario with the private business scenario, as well. There is no distinction, he says:

> Just as no one has a right to enter my home, so no one should have a right to stay at my inn, hotel, or motel; eat at my restaurant, cafeteria, lunchroom, or lunch counter; enjoy a beverage at my soda fountain; fill up at my gas station; view a movie at my theater; listen to a concert in my hall; or watch a sporting event at my arena or stadium.[9]

This notion is difficult to accept today because our society teaches us that racial discrimination is wrong. And I completely agree! Racism is morally wrong and thus deplorable. The problem is: When government interjects itself and tells a private business owner with whom he or she can associate on his or her own property—that becomes a constitutional and legal problem that could generate far more harm to natural rights than the owner of a movie theater could. It is not the government's job to insert itself in this manner. It is the government's job to protect the voice and actions of the unpopular opinion. It just so happens that the racist is in the minority here. The pacifist, agriculturalist, Jew, or Scientologist may be in the minority next time. Roger Pilon at the Cato Institute explains, "We do not all agree on 'the good' . . . one person's 'irrational' discrimination is another's perfectly reasonable decision."[10] It may feel like the world is upside down when we are defending the racist, the misogynist, or the homophobe, but the Rule of Law is in place to protect the minority from the tyranny of the majority.

The (In)consistency of Governmental Intervention

As we have seen, because we have the right to associate, we also have the right to discriminate. Ignoring these freedoms, the government chooses to circumvent our natural rights all the time, combating discrimination in the form of anti-discrimination laws at the local, state, and federal levels. As a result of these regulations, free individuals are required to associate with *everyone*. Again, we call this forced association, and forced association is unnatural and unconstitutional. In its quest to eliminate discrimination, the government violates our rights and is wholly inconsistent in the process. It only mandates that we associate with everyone in theory. The state makes exceptions to these anti-discrimination laws all the time.

Take professional sports, for example. Why isn't the government forcing the National Football League (NFL), Major League Baseball (MLB), or the National Basketball Association (NBA) to add women to their all-male rosters? If the government is so committed to eliminating discrimination, it should be consistent across the board. If the government can force Mrs. Murphy to serve Asians, Italians, and blacks at her Irish pub, the government should force three of the biggest industries in America to eliminate their own gender-based discrimination. It won't.

Why does the government allow these private organizations to discriminate? Are professional sports associations sacred cows? Are they the untouchables? Why is the government making exceptions for them? If these private teams and organizations have the right to discriminate against women and to associate with men only, should not other corporations and groups be allowed the same liberty—to associate with whom they please?

In a word, absolutely! The NFL, MLB, and NBA must have the right to discriminate against women because they are private entities. People tune in to professional football, baseball, and basketball to watch men who are at the top of their games compete against one another. As a result of this choice, the NFL, MLB, and NBA discriminate against women, and that is their First Amendment–protected right. Private businesses have that freedom, and the government must not interfere. However, the state must be consistent and allow Mrs. Murphy the same right.

The Government Does Not Have the Right to Discriminate: Jim Crow, Anyone?

Unlike free individuals and private businesses, the government does not have the right to associate (and alternatively, to discriminate) because it is constrained by the United States Constitution. Specifically, it is limited by the Equal Protection Clause of the Fourteenth Amendment. Instead, the government has been entrusted with the role of ensuring that all individuals are equally treated by the government under the Rule of Law.

In his dissent in *Plessy v. Ferguson* (1896), Justice John Marshall Harlan boldly wrote, "Our Constitution is color-blind, and neither knows nor tolerates classes among citizens."[11] Simply stated, the government cannot pick and choose with whom it associates; and it cannot pick and choose with whom *others* associate either. These are not the concerns of the government. Rather, the government exists to protect our rights; the right to associate *and* the right to discriminate.

Regrettably, in *Plessy*, the majority held constitutional a Louisiana law mandating "separate but equal" train cars for blacks and whites, thereby violating the freedom of association of passengers and the railroad owners. In order to comply with state law, white business owners had no choice but to fund and maintain four train cars—black non-smoking, white non-smoking, black smoking, and white smoking. Private enterprise did not wish to make that decision and incur that expense (rather, it wanted its cars integrated), but the government mandated segregation of the cars, thereby violating all parties' freedom to associate. Unfortunately, the state has failed to protect this freedom time and time again throughout history.

Jim Crow laws—legally mandated discrimination—were the sad and unforgivable result of the Civil War and Reconstruction. These rules and customs and regulations legally enshrined blacks as second-class citizens for years. In my book *Dred Scott's Revenge: A Legal History of Race and Freedom in America*, I document some of the disgusting and demoralizing government-mandated rules that will forever taint our nation's history and that to this day impair the quiescence of American blacks.

In Alabama, for example, it was a crime for blacks and whites to play cards at the same table or walk down the same sidewalks. In privately owned factories, blacks and whites were required to look out different windows. As witnesses in court, blacks and whites had to swear on different Bibles. Black barbers could not give white people haircuts. Blacks and whites had to check out books in separate library branches. This system of legalized segregation was fully in place by 1910 in every state in the South. In the passage of these dreadful Jim Crow laws, the government singlehandedly stripped blacks and whites of the freedom to associate with whom they pleased.

Take note once more: Jim Crow laws were written, implemented, and enforced by the government. They were not the result of free individual action. Private streetcar companies in Augusta, Houston, Jacksonville, Mobile, Montgomery, and Memphis were not racially segregated during the late 1800s. But, by the early 1900s, the railcars were segregated because city ordinances and state statutes mandated racial separation in public accommodations. Therefore, the racists were not the white railroad owners—the racist was the state!

In fact, many companies—including private railroads, for example—refused to adhere to Jim Crow laws. Economic historian Dr. Jennifer Roback argues that private railroads did not want to be segregated but were required to do so by law. Why did these private companies take that position? Because Jim Crow legislation was interfering with their right to run their businesses! Jim Crow legislation was interfering with their freedom to associate and to conduct business with whom they pleased! Just as blacks could not associate with whites in both public and private places, whites could not associate with blacks. So, the railroads objected. One railroad company, the Mobile Light and Railroad Company, "flat out refused to enforce" the Mobile, Alabama, segregation law.[12] It is simple economics and business practice to integrate; it is far more costly to maintain and run four railway cars than two railway cars.

So, it was not the free markets of the South that perpetuated racism. It was the government working in conjunction with racist individuals to "intimidate those who would have integrated" that perpetuated racism.[13] Jim Crow is a clear demonstration that we simply cannot trust the government to decide what discrimination is acceptable and what discrimination is deplorable. We, as free individuals, must have the right to associate, voice our opinions, and act according to our value systems, allowing conversation, discourse, and free markets to weed out the unacceptable beliefs in society.

The government is wholly irrational, inconsistent, and arbitrary as exhibited in the implementation of Jim Crow laws across the South. With its irrationality, inconsistency, and arbitrariness, the government comes up with some pretty nonsensical outcomes. Jim Crow laws merely demonstrate how the government will continue to disappoint in its ability to protect the freedom of association.

Looking into the next century to demonstrate how private companies can successfully abolish segregation without the "help" of the government: In 1947, the Brooklyn Dodgers integrated on their own timing and accord. The fact that this team voluntarily quashed segregation earlier than the rest of the MLB is testament to its success, winning six pennants between 1947 and 1956, with the help of Jackie Robinson. The takeaway here is: The state is not the answer to abhorrent racist behavior. Let individuals and private businesses express themselves! Wrongs *will* be righted. Individuals and businesses will protest the injustice. Individuals and businesses will denounce and reject racist, misogynist, and homophobic behavior. Individuals and businesses will criticize loudly. But the single fact remains: If we are truly a free society, we must have the full right to associate or not to associate with whomever we please—and that means people have the right to be racist.

The Civil Rights Act of 1964 and Private Property

The Civil Rights Act of 1964 prohibits the state and the federal government from making decisions based on race and from enforcing decisions based on race. The impetus for the Civil Rights Act was Jim Crow—government-mandated and government-enforced racism. At the time, the state's invasive hand had, once again, violated the individual's freedom of association, and the Civil Rights Act was central to the abolition of racist and unconstitutional Jim Crow.

However, while the eight parts of the Civil Rights Act that restrain the government itself are crucial and constitutional, two provisions of the Act violate the fundamental rights of individuals—the freedom of association and basic property rights. The unconstitutional provision, Title II, prohibits private persons from making decisions based on race with respect to their *private property* when that property has become a public accommodation, one to which the public is invited in order to conduct commercial transactions with the property owner.

The government does not have the authority to tell an individual how to run his business—who he allows in, who he sells to, or how he manages his finances. After all, what is the difference "between a homeowner inviting the public (minus blacks and Catholics) to his Friday night parties and a businessman who invites the public (minus blacks and Catholics) to purchase his goods?"[14] There is no difference whatsoever. We may not agree with this business owner, but the government must defend the individual's right to run his business the way he chooses. It is his property and his business. This concept is grounded in private ownership rights, elemental tenets of the purpose of government in a free society, and the natural freedom of association.

Moreover, these laws become even more invasive because it is so difficult to determine if someone had the actual intent to discriminate. To address this difficulty, enforcers of the law devised the following rule: Lack of diversity in the workplace (or amongst customers) creates a rebuttable presumption that discrimination has occurred. In other words, once this lack of diversity has been documented, the burden is on you, as the employer, to prove that you did not in fact discriminate. Ironically, an employer could avoid these types of lawsuits by doing precisely what the Act forbade: Discriminating. All you would have to do to achieve a diverse workforce is to hire people on the basis of their race.

More pragmatically, Congress lacks constitutional authorization to regulate private enterprises which do not participate in business across state borders. The Civil Rights Act was passed under the auspices of the Commerce Clause, which expressly grants Congress only the power to regulate *interstate* commerce, that is, commercial activity that takes place in more than one state. The difficulty with the Civil Rights Act is that the vast majority of enterprises it regulates are small, local outfits which have no intention of expanding the scope of their businesses beyond their towns, much less their states.

In order to uphold the constitutionality of the Civil Rights Act, the Supreme Court has expanded its reading of the Commerce Clause to encompass nearly any activity (indeed it is difficult to envision an activity it would not reach). Take, for example, the case of *Katzenbach v. McClung* (1964). *Katzenbach* involved a small barbeque restaurant in Birmingham, Alabama, which had refused to seat African American customers. About half of its food was purchased from an in-state distributor, which had in turn sourced that food from out of state. Nearly all of its customers were locals.

The Supreme Court nonetheless held that the Civil Rights Act was constitutional as applied to that restaurant, due to its indirect sourcing of food from out of state. Because racial discrimination could lessen the total amount of food sold, meaning less business for out-of-state food sellers, Congress had a "legitimate" interest in eliminating this economic "burden." As an initial matter, it should be clear that securing additional business for out-of-state enterprises was certainly not Congress's motivation in passing the Civil Rights Act (at least one should hope not); the Supreme Court is effectively "inventing" a rationale for the legislation. More importantly, this reading of the Commerce Clause has meant that Congress can regulate nearly any activity for any reason it chooses. Ask yourself the following question: How many states (and countries) were involved in producing the clothes you are wearing, the food you have eaten today—even the paper this book is printed on? With *Katzenbach's* jurisprudence, we are no longer a government of limited powers.

This topic brought Rand Paul, M.D., into some controversy on MSNBC's

"Rachel Maddow Show" shortly after his 2010 Republican primary win for the U.S. Senate in Kentucky. Dr. Paul—now Senator Paul—stated that he supported most parts of the Civil Rights Act, except one—Title II. This statement sent politicians and the media into an uproar. Title II makes it unlawful for private businesses to discriminate against customers based on race. Dr. Paul and libertarians everywhere believe that the Natural Law is colorblind, that the personal decisions based on race are invidious and perfidious; but they also believe that the government has no right to force private persons or businesses (nongovernmental actors) to associate with whom they do not desire because this coercion violates First Amendment rights. The net result of the Civil Rights Act is forced association, which is unconstitutional on its face. Neither mandatory segregation nor mandatory association is consistent with the Natural Law or the Constitution in our free society.[15]

The *Washington Post* described Dr. Paul's comments on the cable network as "an uncomfortable conversation about the federal government's role in prohibiting racial discrimination and about a period of history that most politicians consider beyond debate."[16] It is depressing that we, as a society, cannot stomach a conversation on the fundamental freedom of association, property rights, and race in our allegedly "post-racial society."

How Laborious! Labor Unions and the Denial of the Right to Associate

Throughout history, there is a constant and sorry trend of government attempting to fix a problem, inevitably exacerbating the problem, and ultimately violating personal freedoms in the process. In the wake of severe economic troubles during the Great Depression, Congress passed the National Labor Relations Act (NLRA), also called the Wagner Act. At the time, unemployment was high, and the standard of living was declining quickly. In theory, the Act "encourage[s] a healthy relationship between private-sector workers and their employers, which policy makers viewed as vital to the national interest." *Healthy relationship* is a relative term. This particular definition came from the National Labor Relations

Board (NLRB), which is the federal agency the NLRA created. It seems to me that a forced relationship (or association) is anything but healthy. Rather, this toxic federal law is a prime example of forced association in every way, with each and every party affected negatively. Let's start from the top.

Firstly, the NLRA requires private employers to work with certified unions (that are certified not by a neutral third party, but by the government). In doing so, the government is limiting the means by which private employers work and relate with their very own employees. Collective bargaining becomes the rule without the consent of one of the parties, the employer itself. "In ordinary contract law and on the basis of freedom of association, any contract between A and B that is the result of either A or B being forced to bargain with the other is null and void."[17] The government seems to ignore these established legal principles. Through the NLRA, it grossly violates the private property of the business owner and subsequently demolishes its right of association.

Ironically enough, the NLRA also violates the associational freedoms of the very individuals it seeks to protect: The individual workers. Their rights are violated in two ways. First, when a union has been approved by the majority of workers at a company as the "bargaining agent," that union becomes the sole bargaining agent for all workers. It is the voice both of those who voted to join the union and those who voted against the union.[18] As a result, a monopoly develops, and individual workers are barred from even representing themselves; they have been forced to associate with the majority.

Secondly, the NLRA compels the workers to pay union dues whether or not they voted for the union in the first place.[19] The concept is called *union security*, but it is simply *forced association*.[20]

And lastly, the unions themselves endure forced association in yet a different manner. Unions must associate and accept as members any individual workers who wish to join, even those who hate unions, or may cause them harm. Also, if the employer wishes to bargain, the union is obligated to do so "under the principle of mandatory good-faith bargaining" (although this forced association tends to work in the union's favor).[21]

The NLRA violates the rights of all parties involved, stripping them of their freedom of association. Not a single entity—employer, individual worker, or union—has the right to associate with the entity or individuals of its choosing. It is amazing how the NLRA managed to hit so many birds with one stone. As you can see, "the authors of the U.S. Constitution would have considered the NLRA unconstitutional on its face."[22]

There is *one party* that benefits from this forceful, freedom-negating federal regulation: The government. As a result of this labor union–private employer arrangement, the state grows in power, asserting a substantial amount of authority over the private sphere.

Professor Charles Baird poses a solution to the government's obsession with coercion and its tendency to violate the freedom of association: "If Congress insists on giving unions special privileges of coercion, it should be honest and promulgate a constitutional amendment that says freedom of association does not apply in labor markets. Don't hold your breath."[23] When was the last time the government was honest with you?

Conclusion

Court orders can't make the races mix.

—ZORA NEALE HURSTON

A folklorist associated with the Harlem Renaissance, Zora Neale Hurston was a preeminent author of the twentieth century most famous for her novel, *Their Eyes Were Watching God*. She staunchly opposed governmental intervention when the result was any kind of violation of individual freedoms. Even as a black woman, she stayed true to her belief that national law should be colorblind and went so far as to oppose government-mandated racial integration in schools because she respected the freedom of association and believed the state should never have a role in violating personal rights. Zora Neale Hurston knew laws should not be enforced based on an individual's race, but rather decisions, such as association, must be left up to individuals to make for themselves, whether based or not based on another's race. She believed integration would never be successful under the forcible hand of the state; rather, segregated schools would become equal when people personally decided to integrate.

Zora Neale Hurston was so true to her convictions and belief in freedom that she vehemently disagreed with the Supreme Court's *Brown v. Board of Education* decision in 1954 mandating the racial integration of government-owned schools. She even wrote a letter to the *Orlando Sentinel* entitled, "Court Order Can't Make the Races Mix." Not trusting the government to help black America, she continually questioned, "How much satisfaction can I get from a court order for somebody to associate with me who does not wish me near them?" Just as Zora Neale Hurston espoused: The federal government cannot solve our problems, the South's, or anyone else's for that matter. We must be free to associate with those we choose, and the rest is up to time, education, and free market principles.

How dedicated is the government to the freedom of association? Professor Walter E. Williams suggests a test:

> The true test of one's commitment to freedom of association doesn't come when he permits people to associate in ways he deems appropriate. It comes when he permits people to voluntarily associate in ways he deems offensive.[24]

Unfortunately for us, the freedom of association is just one more test the government has failed.

Chapter 5

You Can Leave Any Time You Want:

The Freedom to Travel

Steve Bierfeldt, the Director of Development for Ron Paul's Campaign for Liberty, had a particularly frustrating day of travel on March 29th 2009 after attending his organization's regional conference in St. Louis. There, he sold Campaign for Liberty items, such as conference tickets, bumper stickers, T-shirts, and books.[1] Transporting more than $4,700 in cash and checks from merchandise sales, Bierfeldt traveled from downtown St. Louis to Lambert-St. Louis International Airport with the intention of returning to Washington, D.C. The government, however, had another idea.

Transportation Security Administration (TSA) officials detained Bierfeldt for further screening when they discovered a metal box in his luggage containing a large amount of cash and checks. The TSA is an agency of the U.S. Department of Homeland Security, and according to its Web site, "protects the Nation's transportation systems to ensure freedom of movement for people and commerce." Bierfeldt might not agree with that last part. TSA agents interrogated Bierfeldt for over a half hour and would not allow him to continue to his gate until he answered some very directed questions: "Where do you work?" "What are you planning to do with the money?" "Where did you acquire the money?" Although having nothing to hide, Bierfeldt, in an effort to maintain his privacy, refused to answer the questions. The officers retaliated by further detaining him and asking viciously demeaning questions. As far as they were concerned,

Bierfeldt could be prevented from moving freely so long as he refused to answer every prying inquiry they might conjure up. To them, if he wished to keep his privacy, then he should have wallowed in the safety of his own home. Bierfeldt never answered their questions, and they eventually let him go in time to catch his flight.

As terrifying as it is to envision a world where authority figures could detain and question us for nearly any reason they chose, consider the further effects of this policy. Bierfeldt, if he valued his privacy above all else and, therefore, stayed huddled in his home, would no longer be in a position to pursue his lawful employment as a Director of Development for Dr. Paul. Furthermore, he would also no longer be free to express his political views by participating in and advocating the Campaign for Liberty's values. Still further, if individuals such as Steve Bierfeldt were forced to stay at home in order to keep their privacy and dignity, then the public would lose all access to these political ideas. Stated simply, the government could eviscerate constitutional rights simply by burdening the ability to travel of those whose ideas it hates or fears.

A companion phenomenon now becoming apparent is the resort by the President to ruling by decree—and the people's general acceptance of it. I speak, of course, of the decision by the Obama administration to purchase from former members of the Bush administration so-called back scanner X-ray machines for use at airports. These devices, which cannot detect small amounts of plastic explosive on the skin or anything, plastic or metal, hidden in a body cavity, nevertheless give the false impression of enhancing the safety of the flying public because of the lurid, graphic, even pornographic nature of the digital images they produce.

The government, in order to induce the public into a sheep-like, dazed-infused, knee-jerk acceptance of the porn scanners, offered an alternative even more invasive, unconstitutional, and odious: A public zipper-opening, blouse-removing, groping-your-private-parts alternative.

Never mind that you own your own body, never mind that the Fourth Amendment to the Constitution guarantees that the government cannot touch you against your will without probable cause of crime or a warrant from a judge based on probable cause, and never mind that there is no authority in the Constitution for the federal government to protect private property; it has reached its ugly hands and peering eyes and insatiable lust into our trousers as a way to induce us to be submissive.

The Congress did not authorize the porn-or-grope alternative. Indeed, no member of Congress could vote for this and survive politically. And the one who will rule by decree, that would be the President, claims he did not authorize this; the "security professionals" who work for him did so. He is fooling no one. He can stop this with a telephone call. He prefers us to be pliant.

Even in the Bush years, this porn-or-grope choice was unthinkable. Today it is with us. However, worse than this Hobson's choice is the repellant submissive acceptance of all this by millions of innocent flyers whom the government has duped into thinking it can keep safe. Question: Has the porn-or-grope regime discovered a single dangerous item of contraband at an American airport—a box cutter, a handgun, or an explosive—in or on anyone flying in America? Answer: No. But government propaganda works.

As this discussion shows, the right to travel enables the free exercise of so many of the other rights we most cherish, here the right to pursue lawful employment and freedom of speech. We should not have to check our constitutional rights at the curb simply because we decide to travel. Sadly, it is the right to travel which has been most disparaged throughout human history, our country being no exception. If we are ever to be free, then we must possess an absolute, uninhibited right to travel the world free from interference by government.

One Small Step for Man, One Giant Leap for mankind

Of all the inalienable rights we possess as individuals, none is as basic, fundamental, and natural as the right to movement and travel. As human beings, we enter this world bestowed with natural gifts: Two legs and feet, and the muscles needed to power them; or, in other words, body parts the essential purpose of which is to move from place to place. Furthermore, we are given a brain and the undying yearning to discover, to know the unknown, to see what lies hidden beyond the horizon. Thus, a fundamental right of movement is inherent in our very humanity. And after all, although we can become slaves in many different ways, none is more evident than by losing our ability to move about the world as we please. It is altogether fitting that a symbol of freedom is a broken chain.

The freedom to travel is a part of our national psyche. Our European ancestors settled in America because they had the right to move freely from their homelands. The very history and trajectory of our nation's colonization are testament to man's inherent right to movement and travel. We are a country made up of travelers, wanderers, and explorers. Examples span from NASA to Thomas Jefferson's selection of Meriwether Lewis and William Clark to explore the mysterious and unknown lands of the West.

More fundamentally, restrictions on the right to travel connote that the government is the individual's master, and not his servant. As explored elsewhere, the right to own property includes when and which individuals may enter upon our property, and under what circumstances. If the government usurps this ultimate right from property owners, or grants itself a monopoly over certain modes of travel, then clearly the rights of individuals extend only so far as the government, and no one else, wills them. Thus, circumvention of the right to travel is particularly antithetical to the Natural Law, and the principle that the temporal is always subject to the immutable. *Freedom subject to the government's whim is no freedom at all.*

The importance of the freedom to travel, however, extends much further than the ability to go where one desires. As mentioned before, movement is essential to the existence and recognition of *other* inalienable rights. If you are prevented from leaving your home, your speech is automatically repressed. If you are not permitted to travel, you are kept from practicing your religion in a community of believers. As a result, you are restricted from selecting who you meet, who you marry, and whether you have children with whom you associate. You are held back from potential employment opportunities and prevented from receiving the education you desire. Stated simply, the right to move and be present is inextricably linked to a host of other fundamental rights that you possess as a free individual. Liberty, at its core, is encompassed in the right to leave the place of repression. As Professor Randy Barnett notes, if one wishes to discover which nations offer the best protection of natural rights, one only need observe the direction of the flow of refugees.

The Freedom to Travel in American Law

American courts have, at least in theory, declared the freedom to travel to be near absolute (how they actually apply the right is a separate issue to which we will turn our attention later). The right to travel is so basic to our nature that the Founding Fathers did not believe it needed to be documented in the text of the Constitution. In *Saenz v. Roe* (1999), the Supreme Court stated,

> We need not identify the source of [the right to travel] in the text of the Constitution. The right of free ingress and egress [to enter and leave] to and from neighboring states which was expressly mentioned in the text of the Articles of Confederation, may simply have been conceived from the beginning to be a necessary concomitant of the stronger Union the Constitution created.[2]

In other words, the right to travel is simply implicit in the concept of freedom, and indeed in the Constitution itself.

To further illustrate this point, consider the original meaning of Congress's authorization to regulate interstate commerce: To keep commerce between the states regular. Indeed, the principal reason for the Constitutional Convention was to establish a central government that would prevent ruinous state-imposed tariffs that favored in-state businesses and impeded the natural flow of goods and services across state borders. Thus, the central purpose of the Commerce Clause was to secure, not inhibit, the free travel of goods. If this was the Founders' attitude toward commerce (goods owned by individuals), then they most certainly would have held a similar view on the freedom of individuals themselves to travel.

In more recent times, the United Nations, of which the United States is a member, adopted the Universal Declaration of Human Rights, which provides for a similar right to travel on an international scale: "Everyone has the right to freedom of movement and residence within the borders of each State. Everyone has the right to leave any country, including his own, and return to his country." This is significant for a number of reasons. First, it is further evidence of the absolute and universal nature of the right to travel. Second, it imposes upon the United States an international legal obligation not to inhibit travel within its borders, or to prevent individuals from leaving or coming back.

The Supreme Court of the United States formally recognized the freedom to travel as a fundamental right in *Shapiro v. Thompson* (1969).[3] This particular case examined statutes that denied welfare assistance to residents who had not resided within their jurisdictions for at least one year. The Court held these laws to be unconstitutional because they inhibited migration and restricted movement. The majority wrote, "The constitutional right to travel from one State to another . . . occupies a position fundamental to the concept of our Federal Union. It is a right that has been firmly established and repeatedly recognized."[4] The government simply cannot "chill" travel, as the federal police officers so egregiously did to Steve Bierfeldt.

Doctrinally, the right itself can be separated into three constituent parts. First, taken from Article IV, Section 2, Clause 1 of the Constitution, a person from state A who is temporarily visiting state B has the same "Privileges and Immunities" of a state resident. Second, an individual may move freely between states. Third, when an individual establishes residency in a new state, he or she enjoys the same rights and benefits as other individuals who have been there for years. Together, these components ensure that the individual can fully enjoy an uninhibited, natural right to travel. How faithful the government has been in following these principles is a separate issue to which we now turn our attention.

Physical Restrictions on Travel

On September 12th 1986, New Jersey law enforcement officials stopped Frank Barcia and Alphonse Siracusa during the height of rush hour at a police roadblock on the George Washington Bridge spanning from New York City to Fort

Lee, New Jersey. The stated purpose of the roadblock was to detect persons under the influence of drugs or alcohol or transporting drugs. As would seem obvious to even the casual observer, the roadblock caused massive delays and traffic stalls. Captain Robert Herb of the Bergen County Police Department, who was the highest-ranking uniformed officer supervising the roadblock, testified himself that as a result of this roadblock, over one million motor vehicles came to a complete stop; or in other words, more than one in three hundred Americans—in some cases for in excess of four hours.

Most infuriatingly, a woman was forced to give birth on the shoulder of the West Side Highway in New York City, without the benefits of advanced medicine that a hospital would provide. People were prevented from returning home, from attending work, and from seeking proper medical treatment, all so the police could identify individuals carrying drugs. If we as Americans possess an unconditional right to travel freely, how are these government actions allowed to take place? Shouldn't mothers in labor have a constitutionally protected freedom to travel to a hospital to give birth? By engaging in such police stops, the government is making a calculated decision that we the people are better off not making and executing decisions regarding where we should be going and what we should be doing.

Despite the seemingly absolute treatment of the right to travel by the Founders and the Supreme Court, sadly it is the right to travel which has been most victimized throughout our history. As noted before, the American system of slavery, in which slaves were confined to their owners' plantations, is the most egregious restriction on the freedom to travel. Even the Constitution (Article IV, Section 2, Clause 3) itself enshrined this circumscription of the freedom to travel by requiring that escaped slaves be returned to their "owners": "No Person held to Service or Labour in one State, under the Laws thereof, escaping into another, shall, in Consequence of any Law or Regulation therein, be discharged from such Service or Labour, but shall be delivered up on Claim of the Party to whom such Service or Labour may be due."

Nor did the freedom to travel become absolute with the passage of the Thirteenth Amendment, which formally abolished slavery. During the height of World War II, the Supreme Court upheld the internment of Japanese American citizens in *Korematsu v. United States* (1944). In 1942, President Roosevelt issued an executive order which granted military officers the power to "prescribe military areas [from] which any or all persons may be excluded, and with respect to which, the right of any person to enter, remain in, or leave shall be subject to whatever restrictions [the] Commander may impose in his discretion." In other words, the natural right of individuals to move freely was subject to the whim of a military officer; there can be no clearer statement of the philosophy of Positivism. Subsequently, the military imposed a curfew on Japanese Americans, and shortly thereafter, the wholesale relocation of many to detention centers. Fred Korematsu, an ardent American patriot, was convicted of violating this military order after he refused to leave his home, as any true American understanding the Natural Law and the ideals of our Founders would.

The Supreme Court upheld Korematsu's criminal conviction, upon a finding of military necessity, namely, "the presence of an unascertained number of disloyal members of the group, most of whom we have no doubt were loyal to this country." In other words, so long as there was some subjective, nebulous threat that our enemies' ideas had reached our shores, the government was justified in detaining every member of the racial group to which those enemies belong.

Even more infuriating, the Court referred to this relocation to internment camps as a part of loyal Americans' duty to their country: "Citizenship has its responsibilities as well as its privileges, and in time of war the burden is always heavier." When the internment camps were likened to the concentration camps of Nazi Germany, the Court quickly wrote off such a comparison as "unjustifiable . . . with all the ugly connotations that term implies." In other words, it was simply assumed that such measures were just, expedient, and proper, and the executive branch was free to incarcerate innocent civilians so long as it could muster up the most tenuous showing of military necessity. Liberty cannot exist, much less thrive, in such a polity. In 1983, Fred Korematsu, the primary litigant in the case, had his conviction formally vacated. His response? "If anyone should do any pardoning, I should be the one pardoning the government for what they did to the Japanese-American people." He is right.

Moreover, physical barriers to travel can come in the form of endangering the act of traveling. This occurs when the government monopolizes the protection of airports, and thus prevents private enterprises from providing a truly optimal amount of transportation security. Business is done better in the private sector for one simple reason: Private businesses will seek to maximize their source of revenue and minimize costs to the greatest degree possible. For example, if an airline company were in charge of its own security, it would ensure it had the most effective, state-of-the-art scanning machines. The company would hire the most skilled and amiable personnel available to run the machines, paying them competitive salaries. Periodically, the company would bring in engineers to monitor the machines' efficacy. The company would test its products and employees to make certain it was not allowing any questionable materials or customers through its security process. And lastly, the company would ensure that its consumers, the passengers, made it through its security lines safely, securely, and swiftly. Without providing these services, an airline would most certainly go bankrupt as consumers chose safer, more efficient means of travel. Today, only the government does this, and very poorly. As Professor Robert Higgs notes, "We need to create an institutional structure that aligns the interests of all involved in airport security, a system that will foster innovation and accountability. Such a system can be created and operate successfully only in the private sector."[5]

The government, however, infringes upon the right to travel when it monopolizes airport security and performs a mediocre job, thus preventing individuals from providing adequate security themselves. To demonstrate the government's inadequacy in airport security: Almost one year after September 11th, with all the security implementations that came with a post-9/11 world, a July 2002 TSA survey of thirty-two major airports "found that fake guns, bombs, and other weapons got past security screeners almost one-fourth of the time."[6] In 2006, the government's own investigators conducted covert security tests at twenty-one U.S. airports. Undercover agents carried the materials needed to create a bomb, including components of improvised explosive devices and common household chemicals, according to a report by the Government Accountability Office.[7] The result of the test? The forbidden materials got past screeners and scanning machines in every one of the twenty-one airports tested. Since September 11th, "hidden weapons and simulated bombs have made it through checkpoints in hundreds of tests."[8] If our own government can get past TSA, surely a bunch of determined terrorists can do the same.

The litany of governmental security failures is long, and the taxpayer bill is high—seven billion dollars annually go to the TSA.[9] The Christmas 2009 underwear bomber is just one example of how security is breached under the "watchful" eye of TSA. Even more, shortly after the underwear bomb attempt, Homeland Security Secretary Janet Napolitano proclaimed, "The system worked." There was "no suggestion that [the suspect] was improperly screened." Allowing a man—with the intent to take down a plane and the materials to do it—to pass security and board an aircraft from Amsterdam to Detroit is the *opposite* of the system working. The underwear bomber was foiled in his efforts only because of the actions of his fellow passengers, no thanks to any government screening system. Thus, not only does Homeland Security fail to protect us; the politicians who run it cannot even acknowledge their failure.

As the examples of Barcia at the George Washington Bridge and the TSA show, the government is still imposing physical restrictions on our ability to travel freely. Although they may not be as conspicuous as internment camps or outright slavery, when a mother in labor is deprived of the freedom to travel to a hospital where she can safely give birth, all for some subjective showing of necessity to prevent drunk drivers, liberty is in exile.

Financial Restrictions on Travel

Although physical restrictions on the freedom to travel might be the most infuriating, the impediments to move freely that we experience on a daily basis typically take place in a more surreptitious form: Financial restrictions. Like freedom of speech, if the right is to attain its true meaning, it must be free from the "chilling" effects of government burdens. Stated simply, financial restrictions deter us from utilizing the right, and therefore cannot be reconciled with the Natural Law, which enunciates not only certain rights, but the free exercise thereof.

Financial restrictions typically come in the form of government monopolization of the means of travel, and the subsequent inefficiencies which inevitably occur when a business entity is shielded from competition. Take, for example, New York City's public transportation system. Interestingly, it was initially a private enterprise that was first to provide subterranean travel to the public. On October 27th 1904, the Interborough Rapid Transit Company (IRT) opened the first official subway system. It consisted of a 9.1-mile-long subway line that connected twenty-eight stations from City Hall to 145th Street and Broadway. Unfortunately for all of us, in 1932, New York's Board of Transportation purchased the IRT in the wave of New Deal politics and became the owner and operator of all New York City subway lines.[10]

Fast-forwarding ahead, owing to an absence of competition and crumbling infrastructure, the Metropolitan Transportation Authority (MTA), the successor to the Board of Transportation, approved a 10 percent increase in subway and bus fares from $2.00 to $2.25 in May 2009.[11] Although this may appear to be a paltry sum, the percentage increase in our transportation costs is certainly more than many of us can expect in our paychecks. Are the subway cars and bus seats any cleaner or better maintained? No; in fact, "the trains will be cleaned less often," says an MTA board member. Will the subway be any safer? No; in fact, the cuts in security personnel made the subway even less safe to travel on. In other words, the twenty-five cents out of each subway fare are the product of sheer government waste.

One may wonder, if subterranean travel was not available to us in the first place, then should not the government be free, if not obligated, to provide us this new service in order to further the public welfare? The difficulty with this line of thought is that individuals, in the form of private businesses, should be free to finance and construct their own means of travel. Could the government declare tomorrow that henceforth, individuals will be prohibited from utilizing boats, unless operated by the government? Shouldn't individuals be free to construct their own boat so as to facilitate travel to wherever they desire? The government's grant of monopoly privileges over a means of travel to itself is always in contravention of the right to travel.

Consider in this regard the government-subsidized railroad system. This behemoth transportation matrix has survived solely on subsidies, grants, and loans totaling more than $25 billion throughout its existence (with that amount growing with the immense bailout payments bequeathed in the wake of the recession beginning in 2008). Despite these handouts, train ticket prices have continued to grow over the years. The *cheapest* ticket from New York Penn Station to Washington, D.C., Union Station is $144 for a round-trip ticket. A quick online search for an airline ticket from New York to D.C. during the research for this book came to a grand total of $139 round trip on JetBlue, meaning it is cheaper (and thus more cost-efficient) to travel on a privately owned airline than on a land-based railroad owned and operated by the government. Until the government has legitimate competition, or abdicates control over transportation altogether, these escalating ticket prices will continue to inflict and restrict your natural right to move and travel.

"Give Me Your Tired, Your Poor, Your Huddled Masses Yearning to Breathe Free."

In 2009, Roxroy Salmon, a married father of five children and human rights activist, was ordered to be deported from America. A Jamaican national who had resided in America for more than thirty years, Salmon had been found guilty of drug possession and sale of narcotics nearly twenty years ago. Unfortunately for Salmon, drug offenses were made a grounds for deportation pursuant to a law passed *after* the commission of his crimes, and the preservation of families could not be considered in making the decision whether to deport or not. According to the government, the interest in keeping families together could not override the "public necessity" of immigration policy. Sadly, this is no isolated incident. A study conducted by the Homeland Security Department showed that from 1998 to 2007, 108,434 parents of American-born children were deported.[12] How can a country which prides itself on a respect for liberty adopt a policy which tears families apart, leaves children without parents, and treats the right to travel as subject to the government's whim?

As the above story suggests, the most egregious violation of the right to travel experienced in recent years is controlled immigration policy. Immigration limitations fundamentally inhibit a person's free will to come and go as he or she pleases. Because the right to move is a natural right, it is not limited to just American citizens. Rather, the right to move is so fundamental, it is possessed by *all* human beings—whether they are immigrants or not. While private landowners have the right to prevent or allow "immigrants" (or anyone) from coming on their land, based upon fundamental principles of property, the government does not enjoy a similar right: To suggest otherwise is to say that the government itself somehow "owns" our country, and possesses property rights to it. Upon what legal basis does government property ownership rest? It can have no basis whatsoever; the government can only vest property rights in itself by providing just compensation. Any argument that the government has the property right to exclude rests in turn upon the socialistic claim of collective ownership.

Moreover, if I am desirous of citizens of another country traveling through my property, say to pursue employment, I should be free to grant them permission. The government cannot limit this property right by circumscribing the right of others to travel freely. If the state wants a solution to the unlawful stream of immigrants in and out of the country, then it can simply abide by the Natural Law and let them enter legally.

More fundamentally, there can be no such thing as American exceptionalism. We, as Americans, are not worthy of life, liberty, and the pursuit of happiness merely by virtue of being born in the United States of America; these rights do not depend upon American citizenship for their existence. They are self-evident. In fact, our nation was built on the promise of freedom, not just to those who were born here, but to all those struggling under the yoke of oppression. America is not a geographical border, but rather an ideal: The ideal "that all Men are created equal, that they are endowed by their Creator with certain unalienable Rights." Jefferson did not qualify this statement by saying that all men born in America deserve access to these rights; such a statement would have been even more ludicrous then than it is now.

Moreover, from a practical perspective, an absolute, uninhibited freedom to travel would not have the "devastating" impact on American jobs that is so often conjectured, so long as it was accompanied by the abolition of the minimum wage. When the minimum wage rises, "some jobs that were worth hiring someone to do are no longer worth filling."[13] As a result, there are less low-skilled jobs available for people who live here legally. Thus, when the minimum wage rises, employers, to cut costs, hire illegal immigrants at a lower price instead of hiring people who live here legally (and paying them the minimum wage). Alternatively, if the minimum wage were eliminated, the opposite effect would occur; employers would pay people who live here legally fair market value—not the government-mandated amount—for the work they do. And as a result, immigrants would be less inclined to move here for fear of not finding work. Congressman Ron Paul explains it this way:

> Our current welfare system . . . encourages illegal immigration by discouraging American citizens from taking low-wage jobs [and minimum wage laws discourage their creation]. This creates greater demand for illegal foreign labor. Welfare programs and minimum wage laws create an artificial market for labor to do the jobs Americans supposedly won't do.[14]

Opponents argue that legalizing immigration will only serve to make our nation less safe. Studies say otherwise. Since 1986, the year amnesty was granted to illegal immigrants in the United States, the U.S. murder rate has dropped by 37 percent. Forcible rape is down 23 percent. Drunk driving deaths are down by more than 50 percent.[15] If these illegal immigrants are so dangerous, violent, and predatory, why are these numbers not going the other direction? Furthermore, "much is made of the alleged fact that 30% of federal prison inmates are illegal immigrants." According to the Bureau of Justice Statistics, the correct figure is actually 14 percent, and most of these immigrants are in prison solely for the violation of immigration laws.[16]

Opponents of open borders also argue that illegal immigrants steal jobs and Social Security numbers, drive down wages by working under the table, and do not pay taxes to the detriment of the nation's budget. These same opponents also assume that tougher enforcement at the border would actually eradicate these problems. This, despite the fact that "strict" border control has been our nation's policy for decades, and has not seemed to work well at all. Locking down the border has not halted the flow of immigrants from the south or the north. Rather, the only effect of strict border control has been the perpetuation of the one-way flow of illegal immigrants, making it more dangerous and expensive for all parties involved. Consequently, immigrants in America are less likely to leave for fear of the inability to return. Consider that thirty years ago, nearly half of undocumented arrivals departed within a year. Today, only one in fourteen does.[17]

Moreover, if these men and women were made legal, then they would not have to "steal" jobs and Social Security numbers, but rather they would have their own. They would not drive down wages by working under the table, but rather would work on the books. They would not avoid taxes, but rather would pay them. The net effect of the legalization of immigration would be positive. Immigrants "would gain more of a stake in participating in and preserving our way of life."[18]

I leave you with an egregious story of travel restriction inflicted by government on the oldest and most aboriginal of Americans: The Iroquois tribe. The Iroquois, who helped to invent the game of lacrosse, fielded a team that was the fourth-ranked team in the world. The team was set to travel to Manchester, England, for an international competition in July 2010. The problem arose from the fact that the Iroquois govern themselves, independent of the U.S. government, and thus issue their own passports. More importantly, these passports symbolize that independence; in the words of one of the players, "it's a huge deal because these visas mean so much to our sovereignty." Before the Iroquois team's flight abroad, the British consulate declined to recognize their tribal passports and informed the Iroquois that "it would only issue visas to the team upon receiving written assurance from the United States government that the Iroquois had been granted clearance to travel on their own documents and would be allowed back into the United States."[19]

The State Department and the Department of Homeland Security refused to grant the team this request. Only after public embarrassment at the debacle did Secretary of State Hillary Clinton finally agree to waive the travel restrictions. The next time you believe that the government has your best interests at heart when it restricts the freedom to travel, remember this story of the government's unjust treatment of the Iroquois Lacrosse Team. Perhaps next time they should carry fake weapons instead of tribal documents, as that would at least guarantee them a one-in-four chance of successfully reaching their destination.

Conclusion

In sum, the urge to move about the world, after self-preservation, is the most fundamental of human yearnings. Although our human desires to think and work hard may be chilled with free speech restrictions and taxation, as animate beings we lose our naturally endowed vitality when the government mandates where we can and cannot go. Thus, the right to travel is not only essential to, but *symbolizes* freedom. Perhaps then it should come as no surprise that curfews, internment camps, and unlawful imprisonment are common denominators amongst despotic regimes. Why erode freedom with the slow but unstoppable tide of indoctrination, when tyrannical leaders can achieve their end goal—complete subordination—much more efficiently with restrictions on the right to travel? Although the government may claim to have our best interests at heart when it commands who may go where and at what times, to grant it that power is to subject our liberty to the beneficence of a government which legitimized slavery for two hundred years. The current War on Terror proves that without the constraints imposed by our withering Constitution, it would continue to do so for many years to come.

Chapter 6

You Can Leave Me Alone:

The Right to Privacy

On a Saturday morning, have you ever found yourself with nothing to do? Maybe you decided to take a trip to New York City and spend time with your best friend from college. Together you visit the South Street Seaport and take in the views of Brooklyn while grabbing lunch. Once you finish your meal, the two of you decide to stroll by the Stock Exchange in the Financial District and then pay your respects at Ground Zero. After an exhausting day, you return to your friend's apartment and realize you left your cell phone on the couch. Your phone shows five missed calls, all from your mother, who has been in a "tizzy" all day because she could not reach you. You tell her to calm down and not to worry. The government watched you all day.

That's right. The government watched your every move while you were in downtown Manhattan. In response to the September 11th 2001 terrorist attacks, the New York Police Department (NYPD) implemented the Lower Manhattan Security Initiative (LMSI). Starting in 2007 (if it was so imperative why did they wait six years?), the NYPD installed more than three thousand public cameras and one hundred license-plate-reading devices. These publicly owned cameras, cameras of private landowners, and the publicly owned license-plate-reading devices are fed into an operations center manned by uniformed police. And while you may try to avoid these cameras by staying north of Canal Street, you're out of luck.

Currently, cameras are being installed throughout Midtown Manhattan. In response to the attempted Times Square bombing by Faisal Shahzad on May 1st 2010, New York Mayor Michael Bloomberg flew to London to take a look at its surveillance camera system, or the "Ring of Steel." The "Ring of Steel" is composed of five hundred thousand cameras capturing an individual's identity (within London) an average of three hundred times a day. Mayor Bloomberg is now hoping to duplicate this Orwellian system in New York and install thousands of cameras in Midtown Manhattan by the end of 2011.[1] However, Mayor Bloomberg appears unsure as to whether this gross invasion of your privacy would work. He stated, "It's not clear that they would have helped in Times Square. Other than if the perpetrator knew there were cameras, he might not have tried to come into Times Square." Despite his uncertainty of success, Mayor Bloomberg and other government officials continuously attempt to convince you these cameras and license-plate readers are there to combat terrorism and protect your safety. Unfortunately, the reality is the cameras act as a government-sanctioned intrusion on your natural right to privacy: Your right to be left alone.

But do these cameras make us safer, or do they only make us *feel* safer, and lead us to believe that at least the government is doing something; or are they just another sacrifice of a fundamental liberty at the altar of government expansion? And if we *feel* safer, but are not *actually* safer, won't that false sense of security (thinking that the government is protecting us when it is not) make us *less safe*? As previously described, when the crackpot Faisal Shahzad parked a bomb-filled SUV in the midst of Times Square, in the heart of New York City on Saturday evening, May 1st 2010, he unwittingly illustrated what little effect these cameras have. Not only did the local cameras fail to deter Shahzad from attempting to murder thousands of individuals; they also failed to identify him. In fact, Shahzad was on a plane at JFK Airport, an hour travel time from Times Square, before the police caught him. Clearly, the cameras in place played no role in preventing an attack. It is impossible for the police to monitor these thousands of cameras in real time and thereby thwart crime. The best they can hope to do is to review a tape after a crime has occurred and maybe get a lead on a suspect. That is not prevention or safety.

Fortunately, other governors in our nation are opening their eyes to